Patience:

Harvesting the Spirit's Fruit

Patience:
Harvesting the Spirit's Fruit

Larry L. Armstrong

FaithProbe

ISBN13: 978-0-9823466-0-0
ISBN10: 0-9823466-0-3

Table of Contents

Introduction

IMPATIENCE is as much a trait in me as it is in anybody. We share this generally negative attribute as a species, and although it's often a detriment, it isn't always such a bad influence on us. Impatience makes you work for a better life for yourself or your children. When functioning as a "left-handed virtue," impatience prompts citizens to advocate for new, fairer government policies. It gives potters a keenness to mold a lump of clay into a beautiful sculpture, or a musician's impatience brings the ability to fashion a cadre of individual voices into pleasing music. Impatience ignites a driving force that pushes you toward good deeds when it's harnessed to positive character traits like a strong intellect or a sense of purpose. These will act as restraints on the harsher side of our human irritability—the rash, impetuous, fussy, and edgy aspects of impatience.

Unfortunately, human impatience also demonstrates itself violently, for instance, when the haste of driving late to an appointment creates a road rage affair on a downtown freeway. Clients are lost to a lawyer before he even meets them, because of an annoyed receptionist. Like a fungus on an ailing tree, paternal impatience overgrows the childhood imitations of a son who lashes out at playmates because his will is opposed. A stressed customer brews an intolerant clerk. Hotheaded impulse makes you raring to go in the wrong direction and leads you into an abyss of disgust with someone you love or into the swamp of anxiety where you imagine non-existent threats to your safety. Impatience can be a bitter poison.

The negative side of impatience calls for patience as a desired counter-quality. When annoyance with a situation or person causes you to display intolerance, hurry or distrust, you need to draw from the cool well of patience the water of clear thoughts and serene actions.

This book is intended to lead you into an examination of patience, and at times its opposing forces, so that you can gain a sharper vision of your busy days and your racing activities. Hopefully, God will allow you to find balance and wholeness as you meditate through the contents. It's written from a Christian vantage point, enriched by the resources to be mined from the Bible, along with the church's theological traditions. The book plumbs the deep experiences of human beings as they struggle with the tug-of-war between impatience and patience. You'll be led to value the tense gestures of God's Spirit as he beckons you to walk back and forth on the tightrope of creativity that patience and impatience produce in the sensitive soul of Jesus' disciple.

Patience: Harvesting the Spirit's Fruit is part of a series of books that explore the teaching of the apostle Paul in *Galatians* 5:22-23, and it's dedicated to those who don't want to be in a hurry, who wish not to create dissatisfaction and distress around them. They're the sort of people who want to see the flow of life as one watches a stream rippling over stones and around gentle curves rather than barreling over uncontrollable rapids and falls. If you're still reading, this book is dedicated to *you*. Enjoy it slowly. Patience will come.

Chapter One

Slow to Anger

The Lord is not slow in keeping his promise, as some understand slowness. He is patient with you, not wanting anyone to perish, but everyone to come to repentance.

2 Peter 3:9

DOESN'T God bug you? I mean sometimes he takes forever! You see somebody whose life has been turned inside out by a terrible spouse or through the careless, malicious behavior of a stranger. Your best friend met a mugger or suffered an accident. Something, anything, rips her apart. She's a faithful Christian, she attends Bible studies as well as worship services, but God just sits there in heaven. No vindication! No consolation! Nothing very helpful. Oh, a preacher visits and prays and says, "Hang in there." But God's inactivity bugs you. The mugger hasn't been found. The other driver isn't in the hospital. When your friend is discharged, she won't have a car to drive, and she'll have medical bills and miss work. She pays a high price for a stranger's greed or his inattention while driving. It's frustrating! Why doesn't God make justice happen faster?

Well, God's more interesting than that. His wrath demands human attention. Hateful, greedy or foolish people are going to have to deal with an annoyed God, yet he always keeps his anger under control. It never runs ahead of his patience. The Lord has the advantage of being outside the constraints of time, which means he can and will work according to humanity's incessant desire to observe minutes, hours, days and weeks. Still, he doesn't have to stay within our calendars. God watches all the happenings of our existence—the blessings, curses, and apathy out of which we creatures build our lives. His contract to be our God isn't hedged by a schedule of our choosing. Not only is God not bound by our clocks; he's free from our self-imposed time limitations, because his blueprint for the erection of the marvelous buildings called our lives requires meticulous thought and precise action. Patience is a tool he uses more often than he uses anger.

When trouble overruns your friend, God takes into account not only her needs, but the requirements of the perpetrator, too. The Lord isn't merely blessing you and those you love; he's taking care of the whole world. And this world is a tangle of interlocking and overlapping relationships between people and events, as well as God's own intentions. Tangents run off from all human and divine activities, and they intersect with other connecting lines that create more pathways of meaning and consequence for God to consider as he works out justice and salvation. The complexities are so enormous that no one less than God himself could work it all out.

Heaven's intentions set up hurdles for justice, too. As Peter told us, God doesn't want anybody to perish. He's the Creator who made both you, your injured loved one, and the fool who smashed her Honda to pieces! He wants each one to come to a good end, not just today but six months from now, and for eternity. While his power to heal works on your friend's broken bones, his Holy Spirit is trying to convict the conscience of the driver whose attempt to dial a cell phone caused the bones to break. He wants the guy to face up to poor behavior behind the wheel and come to his senses. He wants the fellow to amend his life and take responsibility for the mistake.

"Patience and perseverance have a magical effect," President John Quincy Adams suggested, "before which difficulties disappear and obstacles vanish." This could explain why the Lord is frequently more patient than his people. He knows that waiting for a change in a person's thinking and actions is worth the time, and if the wait means he has to endure a certain frustration of his own plans, the Almighty understands that persistence wins out. His human servant's pigheaded character becomes pliant in time; then God's Spirit can further enlighten the servant's mind or soften his heart. So God waits for the obstruction to disappear and the stumbling block to be re-carved into a useful device. He deals patiently, sometimes for a lifespan, while the object of his tolerance slowly comes to terms with the divine will and wisdom.

When sin becomes involved in a bad situation, God's patience is more critical and more active. The apostle Paul helped the Christians in ancient Rome grapple with this balancing act God goes through every time you or I make a choice or carry out an action—and each time we neglect to do what's right and wise. Paul wrote,

> You, therefore, have no excuse, you who pass judgment on someone else, for at whatever point you judge the other, you are condemning yourself, because you who pass judgment do the same things. Now we know that God's judgment against those who do such things is based on truth. So when you, a mere man, pass judgment on them and yet do the same things, do you think you will escape God's judgment? Or do you show contempt for the

riches of his kindness, tolerance and patience, not realizing that
God's kindness leads you toward repentance?

Romans 2:1-4

As we allow God's apparent slowness to establish justice in a bad
situation to bug us, we become judgmental and impatient with
other people who are in the circumstances with us. We fail to
see how much we're taxing the Lord's patience and kindness.
He's trying to lead the person we judge toward repentance. He
wants to turn them around, to spin their offenses away from the
relationship we all have with one another—you and me, "them"
and God. Our intolerance is in the way of the process of
redemption. The Almighty is kind and tolerant and patient, but
we demand fairness now. Our impatience is a weak brick in the
relationship the Creator wants to erect.

And worse yet! We're acting out of contempt! Those who've
slandered, gossiped, deceived or in some other manner wronged
us are viewed as worthy only of disdain and derision. Our
judgment is an affront to the patience of God. The demand we
make for fairness—now!—is an insult to his desire to lead
everyone involved in the quarrel to repentance and restoration.

While God observes the imbalance of his people, he remains
tolerant toward me, toward you, toward whoever is judgmental,
but his wrath mounts up against us. We're on the self-seeking
road of sin, and the road leads to distress and trouble, and
beyond those two hills the trail could lead to a lake of fire. Is
there hope for the one who destroys the good life God wants to
extend? Yes. The hope lies in patience. The Lord is already
exercising his patience, and he calls you and me to do the same.
If we continue to push our private desires for a fairness we
believe is right, rather than searching for the truly just end God
strives to reach, then we'll experience the anger he so eagerly

restrains within himself. Patience in God must be matched with patience from his people.

Patience is an attribute of God's own being. It's possible for his people to be patient, because they were made in his image, and part of the image is his longsuffering, his persistent offering of forgiveness and a new beginning. The slow-moving patience of the Almighty stretches across the Bible from *Genesis* to *Revelation* as the example to his people.

In the *Book of Exodus*, following the golden calf incident, Moses was instructed to make two new stone tablets to replace the ones he smashed in anger. God will again give his law to the sinful people. He appears on the mountain in his glorious person, and Moses hears the Lord's self-description pronounced by the divine voice.

> And he passed in front of Moses, proclaiming, "The LORD, the LORD, the compassionate and gracious God, slow to anger, abounding in love and faithfulness, maintaining love to thousands, and forgiving wickedness, rebellion and sin. Yet he does not leave the guilty unpunished; he punishes the children and their children for the sin of the fathers to the third and fourth generation."
>
> *Exodus* 34:6-7

Slow to anger. There's the patience of God! His finest attributes combine generously to invigorate his patience. Compassion...he understands humanity and feels for his creatures. So he takes his time with them. Grace...he displays kindness and charity toward human beings. Patience is born from sympathy and benevolence. The Lord's fondness flourishes and proliferates when he thinks of Israel. Even though his people are fickle, he is faithful, allowing his love to extend to thousands. God forgives because he is patient.

But grace must be tempered by his wise judgment. Grandchildren and great-grandchildren can suffer because of

11

their ancestors' rebellion and wickedness. I've see this when families instruct their young to be greedy and go for the big bucks, the fine life and the big house, or when they instill the desire to compete violently in sports. Thieves learn to shoplift at home! Parents not only model a lying behavior when they call in sick then take the kids to the zoo for the day, but they teach it directly by writing a false illness report for the children to carry to school and by telling them to stick with the story. Sin is a learned behavior, and God doesn't tolerate it forever. He visits punishment again and again, but some families rarely learn from the repeated reprimands. The Almighty gets angry, but he does so only slowly. He is patient because he knows that those who live righteously produce upright offspring, and grace moves up a family tree as easily as a judgment slides down it.

When a person forsakes wrong behaviors he learned in childhood, the Lord waits patiently for him to substitute consistency for contradiction. In other words, he delays while the person matures. As a Christian, I believe the Almighty wants each person to progress in righteousness and gives an individual time to develop, to mellow and become wiser. Not that he needs to be convinced by the growth of such people in holiness, but rather *they* need time to see it! Their salvation, like everyone's redemption, requires that they come to understand the value of Christ's sacrifice, their virtue and God's patience. But the Lord's tolerance must sooner or later give way to his righteousness. He must judge the deeds of humanity, and those deeds will stand or fall during heaven's assessment day according to whether the people have built with straw or brick.

Though he didn't mention patience, the apostle Paul applied this tension between divine patience and impatience to the judgment God will render upon the work of Christians. He told the Corinthians...

By the grace God has given me, I laid a foundation as an expert builder, and someone else is building on it. But each one should be careful how he builds. For no one can lay any foundation other than the one already laid, which is Jesus Christ. If any man builds on this foundation using gold, silver, costly stones, wood, hay or straw, his work will be shown for what it is, because the Day will bring it to light. It will be revealed with fire, and the fire will test the quality of each man's work. If what he has built survives, he will receive his reward. If it is burned up, he will suffer loss; he himself will be saved, but only as one escaping through the flames.

1 Corinthians 3:10-15

The apostle was discussing the work of other Christians beside himself. Believers in Corinth were dividing over the teachers they chose to follow. Some felt Paul was the better instructor; others preferred Apollos. A few claimed Cephas (Peter) as their mentor. But Paul pointed out that God was at work through each preacher. Paul founded the church and now others were laboring for the congregation's welfare, too. The quality of each builder's work would be judged, not by human standards, but by the heavenly Father's criteria. The foundation was all that mattered—Jesus Christ. Paul was content to let each worker's contribution withstand the fire of divine assessment. The best builders' restorative work in Corinth would not be in vain. The apostle even held out hope for those whose teaching wasn't of the highest quality. They'd be saved themselves, although their labor might prove to be either worthless altogether or of lesser value than some of the others' activity.

Behind Paul's comments to the Corinthians is the patience of God which calls forth patience in his people. The Lord isn't slow in keeping his promises nor meting out justice. His desire is that no one perish; all should come to repentance, and new life. So he waits, but not behind the gray backdrop of the stage. He's an active participant in each Christian's attempts to live well. God endures as his people fail and rejoices when they succeed, and he observes how each foible and triumph fits into his overarching plan. He encourages and assists his people as they take small, flourishing steps, and comforts them when they lurch forward in an unintended pratfall.

"Patience," Edmund Burke declared, "will achieve more than force." The almighty God could demand and receive obedience by force, as many people mistakenly think the God of the Old Testament must have behaved. They look at texts such as the Ten Commandments with its *You shall not...* statements, and they glance at the warnings of punishment when one fails to measure up, and they misperceive the intent. Surely, such a God is akin to the troll under the bridge, demanding and unassailable. But the truth is that God is patient when his warnings go unheeded. For centuries he pleaded with his sinning people through prophets like Hosea, Obadiah, Ezekiel and Elijah. He spoke to them using the poetry of love and lament, the visions of destruction and renewal. Yet they remained unhearing—not everyone—but a majority. Through it all God was patiently building a means of redemption through his Son, yet to be born, but who was often described by the prophets. What he could have achieved by force, the Lord chose to win by patience.

In his first letter, the apostle Peter spoke of God's way of creating salvation in both the New Testament and the Old Testament eras. He wrote,

> For Christ died for sins once for all, the righteous for the unrighteous, to bring you to God. He was put to death in the body but made alive by the Spirit, through whom also he went and preached to the spirits in prison who disobeyed long ago when God waited patiently in the days of Noah while the ark was being built. In it only a few people, eight in all, were saved through water...
>
> 1 *Peter* 3:18-20

The forceful, violent death of Jesus was a human deed more than a divine deed. True, God planned it from before creation, but it was humanity who achieved his Son's death, the worse of all our sins. (Not Pilate's sin, or Roman sin, or Jewish sin—*our* sin, "the righteous for the unrighteous.") But his death had an opposite effect than the one intended by its human perpetrators. Rather than protect God's rule from a misguided human being, which was the opinion his executors held of Jesus, his death brought us to God! The Almighty's reign over human life was demonstrated thoroughly. Prior to being vindicated by his resurrection, Jesus preached to the "spirits in prison," who were apparently those people who died during the time before the great flood described in *Genesis*, "when God waited patiently in the days of Noah while the ark was being built."

In other words, during the New Testament era, God waited patiently through the execution of Jesus, then afterward he let loose the waters of salvation, just as in the Old Testament era, he waited patiently while the means of salvation was being constructed. As God works out his plan of redemption, he always endures quietly the violent ridicule of human beings. He's slow to anger. He's patient. He knows how his affair with humanity will end. Therefore, he can afford to wait.

In the *Book of Revelation*, the apostle John brings together the patience of God and the patience of his people. He graphically depicts Christians who suffer as those who are waiting for vindication—for God's justice on their behalf to happen faster.

> When he [the Lamb] opened the fifth seal, I saw under the altar the souls of those who had been slain because of the word of God and the testimony they had maintained. They called out in a loud voice, "How long, Sovereign Lord, holy and true, until you judge the inhabitants of the earth and avenge our blood?" Then each of them was given a white robe, and they were told to wait a little

longer, until the number of their fellow servants and brothers who were to be killed as they had been was completed.

Revelation 6:9-11

As you and I see our loved ones go through accident or mayhem in this difficult world, especially when they suffer despite their Christian faith, we cry out for exoneration, for heaven's fairness to be expressed. But God's plan is broader than human minds, and he encompasses many concerns as he answers our prayers. There are times aplenty when his goals for all the world, for everyone he loves and whom he wishes not to perish, demand the endurance of his faithful witnesses. Longsuffering, an old translation for the word *patience*, is an apt description of what it means to be a Christian in a world torn by sin, accident and desperate days.

You and I are called by the Lord God to have a share in his compassionate and pain-filled patience as he accomplishes the process of salvation and judgment. This means that those who would harvest this piece of the Spirit's fruit must bear for the world's sake the same burden as the Almighty carries. We must become slow to anger and abounding in steadfast love for those around us who are hurt, afraid, lonely, lost, apathetic and spiritually blind. This is not a simple request made by God of you and me. He knows the depth of anguish we will feel, because he feels it too.

Chapter Two

Unlimited Patience

...I was shown mercy so that in me, the worst of sinners, Christ Jesus might display his unlimited patience as an example for those who would believe on him and receive eternal life.

1 Timothy 1:16

THE guy at work irks the daylights out of you, doesn't he? You know the one I mean. He hangs around everybody's desk, trying to palm off work he doesn't want to do. He cracks stupid jokes because he thinks he's a funny man who ought to be playing a local comedy club on Saturday night. He brags about his kids' accomplishments, or their tragedies, as if nobody else's family matters. Whatever he does, the clown drives you crazy and the rest of the staff up a wall.

You try to be patient. After all, you know you aren't perfect, and you probably frustrate friends and co-workers now and then yourself. But this office jerk doesn't know when to quit, and you do not have unlimited patience. No one in the office expects you to tolerate the inane things the Bozo does. They aren't serene around the guy, either. They don't even try to be nice to him!

Patience: Harvesting the Spirit's Fruit

You've heard their words, the little cuts behind his back. You can't think of anybody who likes him, and you feel sad about it. Maybe that's why he behaves as he does. He knows how much people despise him and conducts himself obnoxiously because he wants to make some sort of mark in the world. At least, the practical jokes let him know he isn't being blithely dismissed. You're learning what Thomas Hardy meant when he called patience a "blending of moral courage with physical timidity." Though you'd like to punch the guy out, you resolve to be more patient, to count down before you blast off. But is it patience or pity that motivates you?

As the apostle Paul began a letter of instructions for his co-worker Timothy, he spoke about Jesus Christ's unlimited patience. He reminded Timothy that the Lord's purpose for entering the human realm was to save sinful people, and Paul indicated how he considered himself the worst of a bad bunch— "the chief of sinners." Paul knew how abhorrent he must have been in Christ's eyes. He was murderous toward those who believed in Jesus. He went to Damascus with the intent of arresting Christian runaways and hauling them back to Jerusalem for trial. Despite Paul's insufferable behavior, the Lord displayed unlimited patience toward him. He confronted Paul, blinded him, then sent a healer to him, just to get his undivided attention. When he obtained his interest, Jesus began to guide Paul into a new life of service for the kingdom of God on earth. Through years of wilderness study, and more years of missionary activity, Jesus whittled away at Paul's poor character and fashioned an instrument that could lead churches as teacher and evangelist, disciplinarian and sage. Why did Jesus do this in the apostle's life? So that he "might display his unlimited patience as an example for those who would believe on him and receive eternal life." Through Paul's reception of his Savior's unlimited patience, Christians then and now have learned how longsuffering Jesus is even with the most unbearable people.

In *Countryman: A Summary of Belief*, Hal Borland wrote, "Knowing trees, I understand the meaning of patience. Knowing grass, I can appreciate persistence."

So it is with Jesus' construction of productive disciples. He knew Paul would bear good fruit, but as with a well-tended tree, Christ would have to exercise patience with Paul. He'd have to prune, fertilize, harvest inadequate fruit for a few years, but in the end he'd receive a bountiful harvest from this new apostle. But Paul was like grass, too. He'd grow fast and lush, green and healthy, spreading across large areas and bringing much pleasure to Jesus. But the Lord would have to be persistent, weeding and liming, dethatching and raking. Both teaching and learning discipleship requires endurance.

Could our discipline in Christ's way be any less difficult for him to accomplish? I doubt it. As I read through the gospels, I see evidence of Jesus' bottomless spirit of patience over and over. Do you remember when James and John, the sons of Zebedee, together with their mother, came to Jesus and asked for spots on either side of him in Kingdom Come?

> Then the mother of Zebedee's sons came to Jesus with her sons and, kneeling down, asked a favor of him.
> "What is it you want?" he asked.
> She said, "Grant that one of these two sons of mine may sit at your right and the other at your left in your kingdom."
> "You don't know what you are asking," Jesus said to them. "Can you drink the cup I am going to drink?"
> "We can," they answered.
> Jesus said to them, "You will indeed drink from my cup, but to sit at my right or left is not for me to grant. These places belong to those for whom they have been prepared by my Father."
> *Matthew* 20:20-23

Patience: Harvesting the Spirit's Fruit

Jesus had recently delivered his parable about workers in a vineyard who received the same wage for differing amounts of work. The moral of the story was *the first will be last* and vice versa. Apparently, the Zebedees weren't listening! They wanted to be at the forefront in Jesus' realm. This must have tried his patience, but you don't see it in his response. He simply asked if they thought they could handle the suffering required, and after they were affirmative, Jesus predicted that the brothers would suffer and said that positions of responsibility and prestige were not his to give. This seems to be a gentle and patient answer to three ambitious followers.

Fresh out of seminary, with friends' predictions ringing in my ears, I thought I'd one day serve a congregation of a thousand members. Over the decades, the Lord has shown me that my place of service—where I am called to be—has been much smaller. Through his patience and steady instruction, I've discovered spiritual gifts that suit me to fewer families, fewer meetings, more time with people, more focus on the concerns of small groups that form the major component in Christian community life. Because of God's longsuffering with me, I became a small church pastor by choice and out of a firm commitment to my first love—Christ himself.

Jesus' patience has always proved hard to rattle on many occasions. Think of the time when a man asked him to charge his brother to divide an inheritance with him. At first, the Lord was a little snippy about the request. He replied, "Man, who appointed me a judge or an arbiter between you?" (Lk. 12:14) But he maintained his patience and delivered his famous parable of the rich man whose barns weren't big enough to hold all his crops. Instead of calling the greedy man a fool to his face, as others might be tempted to do, Jesus addressed the disparaging remark to the character in his story and told the character that his life would soon be forfeited to God. Then, quietly, Christ taught the man who'd asked for unnecessary help: "This is how it will be with anyone who stores up things for himself but is not rich toward God" (Lk. 12:21). Jesus was consistently patient in his times of teaching, especially when the lessons were hard to swallow.

Was he ever curt or short with people? Was there a limit to his patience? In the *Gospel of Mark*, the disciples repeatedly failed to understand Jesus. You'd think he'd allow anger to overcome patience. After he stilled the storm, through which he'd been sleeping while the disciples were terrified, he asked them, "Why are you so afraid? Do you still have no faith?" (Mk. 4:40) They whispered together about who he was and how strange it was to have him quiet wind and waves. Jesus, who might have been groggy since he was asleep just minutes prior to this activity, remained serene and uncomplaining toward the dull-witted men.

When the sick woman touched his garment and was healed, Jesus might have easily become impatient, but he merely asked who touched him. Then he rewarded her faith in him with a public recognition as he extended his peace to her (Mk. 5:24-34). When the people of his hometown rejected him, was he impatient and did he call down a curse on Nazareth? No, he simply observed, "Only in his hometown, among his relatives and in his own house is a prophet without honor" (Mk. 6:4). This seems to be a mild response toward people who were ready to kill him. While the disciples hemmed and hawed over not having enough food to feed a huge crowd, Jesus simply asked how much food was available and from it provided what the disciples weren't able to give. Yet he could have complained impatiently about their inabilities. In discussions with Pharisees and teachers, who failed to understand him, Jesus maintained his patience and explained fine points of the law which his opponents tried to circumvent. When the disciples repeated their failure to understand him, Jesus asked them, "Are you so dull?" (Mk. 7:18) As we read this, we can sense his irritation, but the Lord tolerantly walked the disciples through the meaning of what he told the opponents.

As I study through the gospels, I see times when Christ's patience may have been pushed, but like God the Father, he kept his cool and drew people lovingly toward himself. He was slow to anger. "Patient waiting," Jeremy Collier said, "is often the highest way of doing God's will."

As he did with the apostle Paul, Jesus kept working with his followers to bring them into the light he came to shed upon the earth's disreputable conduct. Why? What made it possible for Jesus to be patient in face of rejection, opposition and human dullness? Was it because he was more than human? Did his divine side make patience easy to display? Such questions lead me to also ask, *Is unlimited patience to be expected of Christ's people? Do I have to be patient all the time? Can impatience ever be a good deed?*

The apostle Paul's character may hint at part of an answer. He understood the value of patience. He told the Roman believers, "Be joyful in hope, patient in affliction, faithful in prayer" (Rom. 12:12). To the Corinthians he said, "Love is patient, love is kind" (1 Cor. 13:4). To the Ephesians he wrote, "As a prisoner for the Lord, then, I urge you to live a life worthy of the calling you have received. Be completely humble and gentle; be patient, bearing with one another in love" (Eph. 4:1-2). Paul's personal experiences in life—imprisonment, hardship, abuse—taught him persistence as he dealt over and over with tough congregations and irritating opposition. He learned the need to endure when afflicted. Christian love, as he envisioned it, is wonderfully expressed by tolerance with those who are loved. Having been a prisoner in more than one jail, Paul was persuaded that patience demanded from him a temperate longsuffering with other believers and with non-believers. The apostle knew the importance of maintaining a patient attitude in life. Endurance and staying power come to those who are uncomplaining and serene. In other words, patience and perseverance must stroll hand in hand down the street.

But Paul's patience was not unlimited. Do you remember his frustration with Peter? The great disciple had come to Antioch and followed the dictates of his own experience and his vision (see *Acts* 10:9-23) by having fellowship with Gentile Christians in their homes. After representatives of the Jewish Christian church in Jerusalem arrived, Peter pulled back from the Gentile believers and drew other Christians with him. Paul was angry over what he saw as Peter's hypocrisy. Years later, he wrote a still hot-under-the-collar explanation of the incident to the Galatians:

> When I saw that they were not acting in line with the truth of the gospel, I said to Peter in front of them all, "You are a Jew, yet you live like a Gentile and not like a Jew. How is it, then, that you force Gentiles to follow Jewish customs?"
>
> *Galatians* 2:14

Paul then launched into a long tirade about the difference between observance of the law and being made righteous by faith. New Testament scholars aren't sure whether Paul's quotation of what he said to Peter ended at the conclusion of verse 14 or continued through verse 21. I think the latter verses may be a paraphrase of what he said, mingled with his understanding of justification by faith, which was a major subject in his Galatian letter. But the main thing to note here is Paul's impatience with Peter. His anger over theological

23

differences caused the apostle to drop his patience on the floor. Usually, Paul is seen to be somewhat proper in this display of anger, but as John Dryden said, "Beware the fury of a patient man." I read Paul's remembrance of the incident and wonder where right and wrong, responsibility and reproach, are to be found. Peter was wrong and needed correction, yet Paul may have over-reacted. His patience had its limits.

This raises a practical question: How unlimited can any Christian expect his or her patience to be? Are there times when impatience isn't sinful? Yes, I believe impatience is called for on occasion. It can even be therapeutic, a healing influence, as I think it was for Peter once he thought about his behavior. He later wrote in his second letter, "Bear in mind that our Lord's patience means salvation, just as our dear brother Paul also wrote you with the wisdom that God gave him" (2 Pt. 3:15). The one who was an apostle first recognized the wisdom in the other apostle's teachings and discovered through them Jesus Christ's patience. But do Peter's words show evidence of a strained relationship caused by Paul's earlier impatience? I'm inclined to think so.

Also, was Paul correct to remain angry about the incident years later? Or was he merely using the memory of his impatient anger to teach the Galatians a spiritual lesson? That's a possibility, yet I sense a latent irritation within Paul's memory of the event. An unanswerable question is: Did the apostle to the Gentiles ever completely let loose of his anger? Did the remembrance of it always raise up a spirit of impatience in him? Maybe. Maybe not. Who knows? Still, it's that *possibility* of lingering anger and impatience that leads us to ask if unlimited patience can be required of a believer? of you or me?

Although Paul was a forgiven sinner, he was not a sinless Christian. He understood and taught the value of patience, and probably tried to exercise it in his relationships, but impatience could get the better of him. Anger might impair his judgment, while it made him judgmental. Under the grace of God, such distressing behavior could be repaired and the effects of impatience could be lessened or removed in time. It might have been good if Paul had heard the advice of a Jewish Christian, James, who wrote: "My dear brothers, take note of this: Everyone should be quick to listen, slow to speak and slow to become angry, for man's anger does not bring about the righteous life that God desires" (Jas. 1:19-20). Impatience in itself may not be clearly and always sinful, but it certainly is wrong if we allow it to be coupled with inappropriate anger or too long a memory or any sinful behavior.

A clown at work or a relative who always torments you or a disobedient and frustrating child may make you irritable and raise up a spirit of opposition within your heart, but what controls your responses to the person? If it's impatience, beware! Not that there should ever be no boundary line for your longsuffering, but be careful of the other emotions and behavior that attach themselves to your heart. In the wrong combinations they can melt your patience and create annoyance, edginess or rash words. You'll regret what happens and the memory of it will be difficult to erase. When you think you're safe, it could lift its fanged head to strike your heel in the future. Learning patience and lessening impatience molds your character into a better likeness of Jesus Christ. Even if your patience is not unlimited.

How so? By teaching you what Jesus taught Paul. Christ was patient with Paul the persecutor of the church, despite his character of being the "worst of sinners," because Jesus was showing pity to the man. He cared about the person behind the transgressions; he wanted to make a better man out of him.

Patience: Harvesting the Spirit's Fruit

Jesus' compassion and mercy toward Saul of Tarsus gently and patiently drew him into God's kingdom and transformed him into Paul, an ambassador of the Messiah.

Your patience may be limited, but it can grow, and it will grow, but only in proportion to your pity—your sympathy and kindness—toward those who upset and irritate you. If you want to harvest this portion of the Spirit's fruit, then you have to care about others as Jesus cares about you. Love is the root of all patience.

Chapter Three

Fruit of the Spirit

...the fruit of the Spirit is love, joy, peace, patience, kindness, goodness, faithfulness, gentleness and self-control. Against such things there is no law.

Galatians 5:22-23

COME on now. Admit it. You were in a checkout line, and the old woman in front of you was counting out pennies and nickels to make the exact change for a purchase. *Why doesn't she just give the clerk a five dollar bill,* you think, *and collect the change we all gather in a day's shopping?* You were in a big hurry. An appointment loomed, and this lady held you up. You were a bit angry, and if she hadn't been elderly, you'd have said something rude in an attempt to move her along.

Well, maybe that wasn't your situation. Instead, you sat behind a kid at a stoplight. He was busy fiddling with his radio or a CD player, and the light went green seconds ago. You tooted your horn twice. The kid made a disrespectful gesture, ripped out across the intersection, and you muttered about his foolishness. The guy behind you tooted his horn twice! Out of your irritation, you joined the kid in rudeness. You felt ashamed immediately, but someone waited at your office, and you needed to scurry in order to get there before he left in frustration. You shouldn't have been impolite to the guy behind you, but the kid deserved the toot!

Impatience is as impulsive as a cat that pounces on your lap from a shelf beside your easy chair. You don't notice it lurking above you. Suddenly, you can't ignore it, and you say or do something you regret as soon as it happens.

Hidden catalysts for intolerance are anger, envy, jealousy, stress, selfishness, or similar experiences. You consider yourself disciplined, able to control bad impulses. Your self-image says you're a kind and generous person, able to wait in line quietly or to sit at a traffic signal without fussing over a minor delay in your trip. But like everyone else, you're probably less restrained than you think. Your better motivations don't always guide your behavior. A focus on personal needs and wants, or on the demands of others, pressures your mind, and before you realize it, your impatient deed is over but not done with. You have to face a guilt produced by the failure of your patience.

Hannah Whitall Smith knew, as every Christian sooner or later learns, this failure of righteousness. In *The Christian's Secret of a Holy Life*, she wrote, "Though my feet often wander from the narrow way, how gently he leads me back, how mercifully he reproves me, how lovingly he increases my strength! How can I rebel against him?" There's mercy wide and free with Christ. His Spirit communicates it patiently to the believer. When you endure a collapse in patience, or any other virtue included in the Spirit's fruit, don't hesitate to pray with Smith: "Oh, Lord, you know the sinfulness of my heart, the pride, the impatience, the indolence, the rebellious thoughts that live there; therefore, I come to you for deliverance from them all."

Fruit of the Spirit

Christians observe Jesus Christ's unlimited patience, together with the slowness of God's anger, and they work at following the divine example, frequently with great success, but not without failures. The quest for a patient character is a serious and satisfying aspect of a believer's spiritual growth. We hear its virtues extolled in Sunday school and Bible studies. Our devotionals often remind us of the need for patience. The preacher teaches us to discipline ourselves through submissive, compassionate attitudes so that we can develop endurance, fortitude, and tolerance. By many means, Christians learn the blessings of a patient personality. Yet we slip on invisible wet spots and land on impatience like a stumbling buffoon.

Paul the apostle included patience in a list he labeled: FRUIT OF THE SPIRIT. He wrote, "...the fruit of the Spirit is love, joy, peace, patience, kindness, goodness, faithfulness, gentleness and self-control. Against such things there is no law" (Gal. 5:22-23). People read this sentence and conclude that there are nine fruits of the Spirit; they take *fruit* to be plural. However, Paul discussed one fruit of the Spirit, a Christian lifestyle produced by the Holy Spirit in every believer. The nine separate qualities combine to form a singular fruit of the Spirit. In other words, God's Spirit enters into you, then throughout the journey of your life as a believer, he nurtures and instructs you in the many pertinent details of becoming like Jesus Christ. The sum of your growth is a spiritual produce, and you see it as you mature in each and all of the virtues that comprise the Lord Jesus' character. Patience is only one aspect of the spiritually mature person you're becoming.

What's this mean? It means that when you received Jesus as Savior, you started on a voyage of discovery. You're sailing to a new world. You have a lot to learn. The nine virtues are being taught by the Spirit who now leads you into all truth. As you

29

follow his leadership and take up the various ministries he gives you to perform across the decades, you become more loving, gentle, self-controlled, and patient. Patience is just one of the lessons you're learning as you serve the Father, Son and Holy Spirit in this world.

The multiple nature of Christian growth—it occurs on more than one front at a time—creates a complex spiritual and moral experience. While ascertaining how to love, you may lag behind in your lesson on peacemaking. You might do better next month at finding the "peace that surpasses understanding," but you'll falter in patience. Yet the failure to be patient leads you into greater skill at maintaining an unwearied, uncomplaining attitude in months that follow. You soon discern the huge amount of strength gentleness demands from your character, and patience expands because you perceive the strings that web together the two virtues. Then comes a lesson in generosity, and you discover other tie-ins with patience. Do you see how the Spirit's fruit is a dynamic forum where virtue and vice debate one another while quality supports quality in a believer's life?

Never forget that one result of the Spirit's education of a believer is occasional failure. You'll crash as much as you soar. You'll be stopped cold in your tracks as well as released to run with an exciting new discovery in your devotion to Christ Jesus. Fiasco precedes success even in pious and godly living. Your conduct becomes like that of your Savior, but because a sinful human nature obstructs the speed of the Spirit's leadership, you must move through times of agonized bankruptcy into other times of mystic delight and perception. What seems like catastrophe and collapse is, under the Spirit's tutelage, development and triumph. Failure, then, becomes a key component in harvesting the fruit of the Spirit.

Unlimited by space or time, the Holy Spirit is infinite in patience and waits long for you to see your mistakes and learn from them. A proverb—I think it's from China—says, "In a battle between stone and water, in time, the water wins." You might be a stone, but the Spirit is water! Soon or late, he'll teach you the lesson your failure in patience was meant to present. After all, one of his major assignments in your life is to polish your character as water buffs a rock.

Seen in this light, patience and impatience become matching puzzle parts. They're complements. They balance one another and harmonize within the Spirit's song as it plays inside your character. The remorse and grief that well up in tears when you confess impatient behavior for the hundredth time are employed by the Master to instruct you in the necessity or the finesse of patience. As the two qualities play against one another for years within your soul, poise develops. The Spirit opens to you the blessed assurance that tells you how to wait upon the Lord, how to trust God's love, how to allow grace to carry you when your intellect says there's no hope. Patience is best learned by dealing with impatience under the Holy Spirit's influence.

Let's think for a moment about the Spirit of God's activities within Christian life and church life. From scripture, we learn about three major roles played out by the Holy Spirit. He's your Teacher, your Comforter, and your Advocate. These aren't his only pursuits within your heart, but in all three tasks, patience is required of the Spirit himself, just as it's required of human teachers, comforters and advocates.

When you were someone's instructor, didn't you have to exercise much patience as he or she struggled through the first stages of your subject matter? Even after the initial lessons were mastered, your student asked an uninformed question, although you'd informed him several times. If he'd have paid better attention, he wouldn't have presented his question. Student sluggishness tries every teacher's patience. Imagine how the Holy Spirit must feel about your slowness to learn the rudiments of spiritual living he's been teaching you for years!

When you were a friend's comforter, wasn't patience a valuable tool? You've seen firsthand how grieving people cannot move forward from one stage of recovery to another without lingering for what seems to you like an interminable time. You had to be patient as your friend worked through shock, denial, and anger. Your patience was pressed by her incessant backtracking and detours. Your love for her kept you going. You were concerned that she survive the loss of a job or a relationship or a spouse or a child. You wanted her to become a stronger individual. "Patience!" You reminded yourself. "She'll make it. Just be patient!" Imagine how your stalls and sputterings in the midst of sorrow must tax the Spirit of Christ, your divine Comforter, as he waits patiently for you to move through life's detailed turmoils.

When you were somebody's advocate, surely patience was necessary as you probed in the corners of a private life to find a way to assist your charge in recovering his righteousness before he faced those who might judge him. Did you help an alcoholic rummage through the reasons why he drank too much? Perhaps you helped a cheating husband figure out why he sought the illicit affairs. You could've prodded a person about bad behavior on the job or with co-workers, fulfilling your obligation to an employer to prepare the offender for a review board or disciplinary committee. Your goal was always to help, to advocate in the person's favor. Your desire was to lead him in his self-evaluation and to forestall a worse outcome when others discovered his mistakes. How patient you needed to be as the individual denied his wrongdoing or misappraised himself! Now consider how patiently your heavenly Advocate walks with you through the preparation for your appearance before God's final tribunal.

In his book *Pleasing God*, R. C. Sproul wrote, "To be a loyal friend requires more than blind acceptance. It requires patience, long-suffering, gentleness, the kind of fruit that flows from the Holy Spirit. It is because Christ is loyal to us that we are motivated to show that same kind of loyalty to others."

The part of the Spirit's fruit which we call *patience* is a virtue that situates a person well for life's expedition through wild lands. Day-to-day experience demands tolerance and serenity which only patience creates. Fortunately, the Holy Spirit is a divine person with infinite patience. He guides you successfully to the safari's end.

As we acknowledged, Christ's Spirit is Teacher, Comforter and Advocate for God's corporate people. He teaches an entire congregation as he instructs you. Without complaint, he repeats lessons about forgiveness. Through longsuffering back-steps as a church learns to be like Jesus Christ, the Spirit leads its people to minister within its neighborhood. He comforts the body of Christ while it struggles through pastoral changes, or the destruction of a building by fire or flood, or a host of other communal upheavals. When church members are overwhelmed by woe and weariness, he's the Advocate who corrects a poor picture of Christ, whether it's displayed to the world by either a local congregation or a whole denomination. The Spirit labors without delay and with unlimited endurance to lift out of sin and confusion all corporate expressions of Jesus Christ's people. He prepares the body religious for its appearance in the Judge's chamber. How patient the Spirit must be!

Trace how the Holy Spirit must have worked tolerantly in the apostle Peter's life. After a miraculous catch of fish, Peter fell onto his knees in a boat and said to Jesus, "Go away from me, Lord; I am a sinful man!" (Lk. 5:8) The Spirit had begun to teach the new disciple about Jesus and himself. When a woman stroked Jesus' garment and he demanded to know who touched him, Peter tried to point out the silliness of trying to identify who brushed him in such a crowd. He didn't appreciate the sensitive power of his Master, so Jesus took only Peter and two other disciples with him into a room where a dead child lay. There he resurrected the girl, and Peter marveled with the others in the house over Jesus' ability (cp. Lk. 8:40-56). How patiently the Spirit instructed the disciple! Following a private prayer time with his entourage, Jesus asked who people claimed he was. Different answers were given, then Peter uttered his famous confession: "The Christ of God" (Lk. 9:20). Once again, the Holy Spirit tutored Peter, who probably didn't yet perceive the breadth, depth and height of his profession of faith. As Christ was this disciple's patient Teacher, so the Holy Spirit also taught him.

Now consider how the Spirit had to be patient when he was Peter's Comforter. Shortly after the institution of the Lord's Supper, Jesus spoke with the disciples about servanthood and about their places as judges in the coming kingdom. Then he turned to Simon Peter. As Luke's gospel reported,

> "Simon, Simon, Satan has asked to sift you as wheat. But I have prayed for you, Simon, that your faith may not fail. And when you have turned back, strengthen your brothers."
> But he replied, "Lord, I am ready to go with you to prison and to death."
> Jesus answered, "I tell you, Peter, before the rooster crows today, you will deny three times that you know me."
> *Luke 21:31-34*

Jesus warned Peter that all the disciples were about to be sifted by Satan; then he gave Peter the vital, frightening task of being the one who'd recover first and so was charged to strengthen his compatriots for whatever came next. Though Jesus prayed for him, Peter was given an awesome responsibility. He must have felt it strongly—the honor and the terror of it. He indicated his readiness. He'd die or go to jail with Jesus! But Jesus deflated Peter's high opinion of himself by predicting his triple denial which was coming later the same evening. How Peter needed comfort! I believe the Holy Spirit was there to sustain him. On Pentecost, Peter told inquiring people what I think he learned firsthand for himself: "Repent and be baptized, every one of you, in the name of Jesus Christ for the forgiveness of your sins. And you will receive the gift of the Holy Spirit" (Ac. 2:38). The Comforter's patience with Peter was well-placed and rewarded.

Think about the continuing patience displayed by the Holy Spirit when he functioned as Peter's Advocate. An angelic visitor communicated with a Roman named Cornelius, ordering him to summon Peter who was being provided by God as an answer to the centurion's piety and prayers. As the man's messengers approached Peter's lodging, the apostle was deeply engrossed in a visionary experience in which God instructed him to eat food he'd never consumed before. He was not to consider what God declared clean to be impure! The Lord prepared Peter for his next assignment—to visit a Gentile and share the gospel with his household. When the vision ended, the Holy Spirit told him, "Simon, three men are looking for you. So get up and go downstairs. Do not hesitate to go with them, for I have sent them" (Ac. 10:19-20). The divine Advocate promoted God's will to the apostle. Obeying, Peter went and proclaimed the good news to Gentiles who accepted Christ as Savior and Lord. A new door opened for Christianity.

Patience: Harvesting the Spirit's Fruit

As we saw in the previous chapter of this book, Peter later went to Antioch and created a problem in that congregation when he refused to share fellowship with Gentile Christians after Jewish Christians arrived from the Jerusalem church. Paul took him to task, and a strained relationship existed for a while between the two workers among the Gentiles. I have little trouble imagining the Holy Spirit advocating God's will with Peter as the apostle labored through this unsettling experience, nor do I have difficulty seeing the Spirit advocating Peter's usefulness to the Father and Son despite his continued failures. I have no doubts that Paul also was disciplined by the Holy Spirit to accept Peter once their tensions eased.

Part of the Spirit's job in a Christian life is to campaign in heaven with God for the believer's blessing, as well as on earth with the Christian for God's benefit. Fortunately, as Oswald Chambers said, "There is no patience equal to the patience of God." The Spirit's heavenly and earthly efforts demonstrate how true this is. He sponsors the practice of forgiveness and instills strength in those who are forgiven. He's your Advocate! And O, how he must be patient! As Peter learned at a snail's pace, so you discover the grace of God active and sharp in your life but only by degrees and haltingly. Bit by bit, the Spirit of Christ refashions you into a clearer and clearer reflection of your Savior. Time passes leisurely as he shows you how the Almighty directs your days and reaps more reward from your service than you perceive. The Holy Spirit must be patient so that you can understand God's ways, which work more slowly than human beings notice. While he does all of this, the Spirit brings God the Father and God the Son an awareness of the success they're having within you.

Patience—part of the Spirit's fruit—is learned gradually, and the Spirit himself is your best example of this virtue. Analyze how he's rummaged through your life in order to find his best opportunities to teach you patience. When did he send delays to obstruct your plans? He was teaching you to wait for God to clear the way. When did the Spirit of God allow someone to provoke you to anger or ridicule? He was advocating the use of God's grace and compassion in your relationships. When did the Comforter soothe your heart after a difficult person upset your day? He was using patience to build up your toolset of Christian virtues.

Writing about the fruit of the Spirit, David Jeremiah said in his book *God in You: Releasing the Power of the Holy Spirit in Your Life*: "It isn't your fruit; it is the fruit of the Spirit. It isn't something you go out and try to do. You can't sit in a chair and try to work yourself up to peace or love or patience or goodness. It grows within you—a natural product of the Holy Spirit living within you. He produces these qualities in your life."

The Spirit's fruit comes as you live though your daily experiences under his guidance and discipline. The harvest he produces within you has a multitude of expressions. Kindness, generosity, faithfulness and other qualities unite to restore the broken image of God in your sin-prone character. You're becoming holy as Jesus Christ is holy, more by your relationship with his Spirit than by your own doing, yet you must cooperate with the Holy One. Patience is the aspect of his fruit that we're examining. So ask yourself, "Have I ever uncovered how the Holy Spirit creates patience within my day-to-day behavior?"

Consider this scenario...

Ahead of you at the lunch counter, the person who asks the waitress more questions than seems necessary about what's on the menu may be there, under the grace of God's Spirit, to foster patience in you. Will you allow the delay in your pressing schedule to irritate you and cause you to miss the Teacher's lesson? It may take a few minutes to learn. Are you patient enough to study this short-lived opportunity to grow into likeness of Jesus Christ? Should you fail, consider this: If you become impatient and interrupt the other person's useless questions, and if you place your order rudely, the Holy Spirit will use the interplay of patience and impatience. He'll couple them with embarrassment and guide you into a holier lifestyle down the road a bit. The Spirit is so patient! And he never gives up on those whom he is redeeming and sanctifying! Give him thanks. He's helping you to mature in the grace of Christ.

Chapter Four

The Immature Soul

The seed that fell among thorns stands for those who hear, but as they go on their way they are choked by life's worries, riches and pleasures, and they do not mature.

Luke 8:14

IN 1519, Hernando Cortez was commissioned by the Spanish governor of Cuba to invade the Yucatan peninsula and capture what we now know as Mexico. He was equipped with 500 soldiers, eight teams of horses and less than a dozen cannons. In a speech to the men before they embarked, Cortez shouted, "We have just our swords and our good right arms to defend us against the savages' numbers. Let no childish strife or disagreement weaken the facade we present to our enemy." In his proclamation, Cortez appealed to the army's Christian virtue. They were going to subdue the savages then instruct them in Christian faith and morals. In this enterprise, which many today consider a venture in hypocrisy, he would tolerate no immature behavior among his troops. There must be patience in the ranks. Personal quarrels and dispute must be controlled, if not by the men themselves, then by their officers.

As Cortez felt it necessary to restrain the natural inclination of combat troops to bicker and disagree over petty things when not busy fighting battles, so too, immature people within the church are required by pastoral exhortation to be patient and not to stir up their congregations.

To the Philippians, Paul wrote about having no confidence in the human nature, the *flesh* as he called it. He talked about outward signs like circumcision, which erected false distinctions between people, reminding the Philippians that he once sought such flesh-bound differences (see Phil. 3), but in Christ he threw all such pseudo-excellence away, like garbage. Instead, he'd forget what lay in his past and stretch out like a runner reaching the goal and the prize that came with crossing the finish line. "All of us who are mature," Paul said, "should take such a view of things. And if on some point you think differently, that too God will make clear to you. Only let us live up to what we have already attained" (Phil. 3:15-16).

What is immaturity? It's a huge blockade that stands in front of patience. Left to our own devices, we human beings often revert to pettiness, silliness and irresponsibility. From a Christian perspective, the biggest brick in the wall of immaturity is sin. Our transgressions make us into hotheaded juveniles, babies in good behavior, demanding our privileges, our desires, our whims. We want our wishes to be placed above all other's wants or needs. Each of us must deal vigorously with the immaturity of our souls. Our sins serve eagerly as prison guards for patience, keeping it bottled up where it cannot express a life-giving witness to God's presence in our hearts.

Look at arrogance. Someone you know has been told over and again how capable he is. Perhaps it started in the home with parents who wanted their boy to grow up with self-confidence and poise. But they were too lavish with their praises, allowing their baby, toddler, pre-teen then adolescent boy to develop a belief that he could do, have, and demand anything. He became adept at manipulating people to get what he wanted, and over the decades he emerged as a business person who could make things happen and command others' loyalty, at least outwardly, so that he achieved his goals. But the cost has been a parallel development of an ego the size of Manhattan. The fellow's smug, conceited and full of self-importance. Has patience become one of his strong points? Probably not. Unless he can use it to manipulate circumstances and gain what he desires. His basic character is a personification of arrogance. When you see him, you see a combination of overconfidence, superiority, and pride that allows no one around him to feel comfortable. Most people do not like the man. They recognize his basic immaturity of soul.

Like many of the wisdom writers of the Old Testament and ancient times, the biblical psalmist considered the nature of arrogant people. In *Psalm* 10, we read...

> In his arrogance the wicked man hunts down the weak,
>> who are caught in the schemes he devises.
> He boasts of the cravings of his heart;
>> he blesses the greedy and reviles the LORD.
> In his pride the wicked does not seek him;
>> in all his thoughts there is no room for God.
> His ways are always prosperous;
>> he is haughty and your laws are far from him;
>> he sneers at all his enemies.
>
> *Psalm* 10:2-5

Arrogant people do seem to prosper, don't they? But not in the treasures of truly good living. Rather than relate to God and conduct themselves by the rules of godly character, the proud person is always bringing up what he wants to acquire or accomplish. He uses other people's greed for his benefit. The Lord is far from his considerations as he plans his activities for the day and the year.

In such an atmosphere, is it hard to conceive of impatience overrunning the arrogant person? Isn't this why some tough bosses are haughty and sneer at employees? Such managers also are quick to reward the workers who are greedy for overtime. They catch them in the schemes they invent, too. I think this is why some clients' bills are padded. Isn't egotism why some business owners look for workers who are willing to cut corners (the psalmist's "weak" people who are hunted down by the arrogant)? Not to mention the boss who snickers at God or things religious. Ask such a bigheaded boss for time off to attend Good Friday worship, and see how his impatience flares. His work is too important to be delayed by your religion! An attitude like this betrays an impatient self-conceit that God plans to judge at the right time.

Patience is also smothered by envy. An acquaintance of yours once seemed to be a good friend, but she treats you differently now that she's gotten to know you well. She started attending a Bible study the same time you joined it. Your interests were similar, and you became friends quickly. Before long, you visited each other's homes, and your children played together. Your husbands were not fast friends but seemed to like each other well enough. Then a distance grew—fewer phone calls during the day, less frequent visits, then silence. You've wondered if her coolness was caused by a fault within your personality. Then you discover the reason when someone else reports your friend's jealousy. She's always desired a home like yours but lives in an apartment on the edge of town. She resents the vacations you can afford, and she covets your furniture!

She's made comments to others about you that sound like spite. You wonder why she carries a grudge when you never flaunted your family's standard of living. Envy is a sign of an immaturity of soul that keeps your friend from establishing a better lifestyle of her own. Her patience has worn thin, and jealousy has pulled her away from fellowship with you.

The New Testament writer James discussed the dangers of envy in a letter.

> ...if you harbor bitter envy and selfish ambition in your hearts, do not boast about it or deny the truth. Such "wisdom" does not come down from heaven but is earthly, unspiritual, of the devil. For where you have envy and selfish ambition, there you find disorder and every evil practice.
>
> *James 3:14-16*

When we want what isn't ours, but belongs to another, our eyes have turned inward, and we see things in our souls we don't want to admit are there, because we think better of ourselves. Yet ambition, like jealousy, easily pulls the wool over our eyes. We want more and more what we covet until we obsess over it. In an inordinate stage, envy starts to resent our neighbor who possesses our precious object, and we scheme about how we might acquire control of it. Or on the job, we desire a promotion or the assignment of a lucrative territory to ourselves, and ambition overpowers an office friendship. Patience between co-workers evaporates and is replaced by rancor and backbiting. We go after a prize regardless of the deterioration of our relationships among co-workers. In the end, the boss discovers "disorder and every evil practice." When she loses *her* patience, heads will roll!

I've seen the movies based on Tolkien's *Lord of the Rings* series of books. (I really should read them!) Anyway, in the movie that focuses a lot on Gollum, the former Hobbit who became deranged because he wore the evil ring for many years, I observe a character torn by envy. Mr. Frodo has his "precious," as he calls the ring. Gollum wants to own the ring again and is jealous of Frodo. His patience wears thinner and thinner as he plots to regain it. He posits murder and connives against Frodo's companion Sam. In the end, as Gollum takes hold on the ring and falls into the volcanic river below him, he loses his grip on the ring, but even as he dies, he grasps for the ring several times. The evil of envy is that it drives a person into deeper sins, and impatience becomes a character trait standing beside resentment and suspicion and avarice.

When the apostle Paul talked about the fruit of the Spirit, he concluded by urging the Galatian Christians to live in a better way. "Since we live by the Spirit, let us keep in step with the Spirit," he said. "Let us not become conceited, provoking and envying each other" (Gal. 5:25-26). The practice of conducting your days based on joy, peace, love, kindness and other virtues— like patience—does not lead to pride and envy, nor to the rehearsal of other sins.

Yet any and every sin will tie up your patience and hold it captive. Examine gluttony. Over-eat, gain weight, and weight, and more weight. Then diet, diet, and gain weight again. That's a pattern of life we Americans (but not us alone) thrash against throughout our adult lives. To what end? What do we achieve by our gluttony and our guilty diet crazes? In my experience, little. Mostly, patience with yourself flies out the window! Or you become irritable and mean-tempered!

But gluttony involves more than food and eating too much of it. Consuming too much of anything is gluttonous. Overindulge in sports, and you become addicted to them. I've been a guest in several households where we played volleyball, basketball and baseball in different parts of the yard. Then we ate picnic lunches, rested, and went back for some badminton, horseshoes and lawn darts. To cool off, we retired to an air conditioned family room where we watched golf and talked about the approaching football season. In the evening, we shot pool, and a few left the party to go to a local raceway. Across America, family gatherings often follow such an excessive model of sports-dominated reunions.

The gluttony of sports is seen in other ways, too. Billions of dollars a year are spent on sports and sports equipment in the USA, and around the world the total must reach trillions of dollars, or Euros or whatever currency you choose. But my point is: Humanity is gluttonous for sports! And such gluttony leads to bar fights during play-off games or to verbal fisticuffs over whose team or which player is the best. The patience of many sports fans wears out quickly. Witness the violence after soccer games. Patience can be scarce in the world of sports.

Anytime we dissipate our energies or become intemperate in an activity which is, in itself harmless or even beneficial, we're guilty of gluttony. And trailing somewhere behind on its heels comes a sidekick—impatience. This doesn't mean sports are to be avoided. The sports-minded person has to control himself or herself, because sin worms its way into the best of experiences. Beware the dangers of excess! Especially if you want to be a patient person.

Materialism is also a vice that robs patient people of maturity and drags them unwittingly into the shadow lands of the soul. Because everyone needs food, clothing, shelter and warmth, we raise in our hearts a desire for security. We want to know there will be enough in the pantry, there will be appropriate garb for work or playtime, and a solid roof over our heads. Out of the desire to have adequate resources, avarice can re-create a greediness for extra of the basics. A husband and wife acquire stock and property, insurance and a savings account, furnishings and toys. These items are considered the necessary foundation for a well-rounded and protected life in an uncertain world, but the acquisition of things can be twisted by impatience. Bad investments are made because sound investments aren't yielding as big a rate of increase as one marriage partner desires. The impatience fuels the poor decisions, then leads to a little shady dealing, a bit of undercover income, tax evasion, or other legal trouble. Proper dreams are unscrewed into an unholy mess because a couple stops being patient.

Those who want more money so they might consume more of the world's goods ought to mull over what the Preacher in *Ecclesiastes* discovered in his search for wisdom:

> Whoever loves money never has money enough;
>> whoever loves wealth is never satisfied with his income.
> This too is meaningless.
>
> *Ecclesiastes* 5:10

Allow your patience to protect you. Wait on God in your need for food, clothing and shelter, and invest your best efforts in meeting life's genuine necessities. Does security rest in things or in the Creator? Believe that the Lord is your only collateral for a good life and act on it daily. You won't be disappointed.

The immature soul is easily led astray. An employee starts off doing a job well because he needs work, an income, but the hectic life of the foundry or the office or the sales floor is boring or non-stimulating. A computer worker glides into minutes of idleness that appear to be busy, but in truth, he skips around the internet avoiding the work he's supposed to do. His paychecks continue so he sneaks more company time to place a personal order for a videogame that will be a Christmas gift, to secure concert tickets, to research a tax question. Sloth and indolence creep in like mice to nibble away at a person's heart for labor.

When the boss notices a productivity slump, he cracks down on the use of the office computers for personal business. And what happens? The laziest workers complain impatiently about the top guy's sternness and insensitivity. "Does he think he owns all our time?" Those who become apathetic about work are often guilty of impatience.

People who fall into extramarital affairs may be annoyed with a spouse. She might be irritated with his inattention to the point of impatience, or he may be edgy with her about bad habits. A yearning develops for whatever a cheating spouse thinks is missing, and its fulfillment is sought in territory that should not be explored. Whether or not the vanished ingredient reappears in the marriage, the adulterous one is increasingly hotheaded at home, and in time probably around the illicit lover. Anxiety and thoughtlessness entice a person into intolerant and rash actions. Affairs are entered and exited to the accompaniment of woeful impatience and immaturity.

Lack of patience can both lead into sin and compound sinful activities in which you're already engaged. As I've been trying to demonstrate, you can take a list of sins and trace through each one the potential motivations for it, and ask where patience or impatience has an impact. Then you discover the connected nature of our human virtues and vices. Strive for qualities such as patience, and you can learn to endure, to persevere, when sin tempts you to stumble or after it has already tripped you.

An immature soul hasn't learned to harvest the fruit of the Spirit, qualities such as kindness, faithfulness, gentleness and self-control. Patience, the subject of this book, is among these qualities that display the presence of Jesus Christ's Spirit within a human being. As you and I learn more about patience and how to achieve it, we're connected to the sinful side of our nature as well as to its righteous side, because patience is balanced by impatience. The two are always in a tense tug-of-war, at least while we live on this side of Christ's coming again. We do not discover what one is without identifying the other, too.

Rummage through your relationships and daily activities, as well as your basic attitudes toward life, work, leisure, children, family, education, church, or any worthy endeavor of the human soul. Delve into anything you believe makes you the person you are, both happy and sad parts of your life. Now assess where being patient helped you. Determine why humble persistence paid off in the joyous arenas of your experience. But don't neglect life's bad times. When has patience assisted you through them? How has impatience contributed its poverty to the situation? Has the interplay between patience and impatience been beneficial or detrimental? When? How? Why? Tear apart one piece of your world at a time, seeking to unearth the buried treasures of patience.

Self-examination will be aided if you keep a private journal or make lists of the positives and negatives you come upon. Your goal in this journey through your experiences is to see how patience and impatience entwine themselves in the sinful side of your nature, and in your developing righteousness. The search may be painful, but be patient and press onward. The Spirit's fruit will present itself in due time.

Chapter Five

The Virtuous Soul

The seed on good soil stands for those with a noble and good heart, who hear the word, retain it, and by persevering produce a crop.

Luke 8:15

COME NOW. Be honest. Do you wish to be known as a virtuous soul? When asked straight out, I find people are quick to answer, "Of course! I want to be a good person." But that's not what I asked. I didn't ask whether you were good or bad. I asked if you wanted to be considered *virtuous*. People hesitate when answering this question. The typical image of a virtuous person isn't appealing. They think of fuddy-duddy individuals who are given to pious pronouncements and picky ethics— Puritans! And most people hope to be known as easygoing or tolerant or respectful, but not overly pious or goody-goody. So tell me, do you wish to have a reputation for being virtuous?

What is virtue? Virtue's a matter of quality, not the snobbish quality of an old aristocracy, but the authentic quality of a high caliber person. The best features of humanity's likeness to God are visible in a virtuous temperament. Such an individual has many excellent assets, and he or she merits the affections of others, whether or not those affections are ever given. A virtuous person is morally upright, a worthy friend, an advantage for any society. Despite the presence of sin in the world, God's image is at the foundation of the human character, and virtuous people allow those finer values to hold sway in their personality and activity. Virtue sometimes seems to be a forgotten benefit in today's world of greed, ambition and lust. Yet the virtuous person is a light for human beings, a signal that calls others to the safety of genuine honor and truthfulness.

Patience is a central quality in the life of virtuous people. It's necessary if you're to learn the evenhandedness, temperance, and compassion your virtuosity is meant by God to display on our murky planet. Virtue is God's intent for our characters, though the behavior of many people tries to dispute God's claim on our conduct. As the author of the *Book of Ecclesiastes* declared,

> This only have I found:
> God made mankind upright,
> but men have gone in search of many schemes.
>
> *Ecclesiastes* 7:29

Why humanity believes self-management is better than God's guidance is a mystery except when our thoughts allow sin to reveal its effect. The evil and malevolence that rise from the distorted side of human nature are motivations for pursuing virtue and value in our activities. And this is where patience touches our effort to follow the Lord's will. Virtue is learned slowly, with multiple side-steps and failings. It can be achieved by youth, but it mellows and broadens with age. Virtue is a lifetime endeavor. Becoming virtuous means being patient and persistent.

As the farmer who plants good seed in good soil, then, you must allow God to sow his word and will in your heart and nurture uprightness in your soul. Work at it constantly, in rainy or sunny conditions, with hope and vigor. Wait, watch, prune, and study each day what you're producing. Remember the promise about the Lord in this proverb:

> He holds victory in store for the upright,
> he is a shield to those whose walk is blameless,
> for he guards the course of the just
> and protects the way of his faithful ones.
>
> *Proverbs 2:7-9*

Let's turn to the practices of a virtuous soul in order to learn what Christian living requires of our patience.

Virtues practiced by a righteous person that are difficult to visualize include qualities like faith, hope, charity, fortitude, justice, temperance, and prudence. They're intangible concepts; you can't touch them, weigh and measure them, or taste and sniff them with your physical senses. But they're experienced with strong emotions and high aspirations attached to them. Through your exercise of patience, they form the core of your life in a tough environment.

In your heart, you understand faith as an abiding, resolute conviction. You also know it as a sincere devotion, a feeling of belonging to Christ Jesus—the object of your faith. Faith was Paul's breastplate, the spiritual armor that protected his soul from the doubts and fears so many people undergo when they encounter anguish in this life. Faith brings you assurance that you're on track with God and with a higher plan for your days and nights.

Faith makes it possible for the terminally ill Christian to get up in the morning. It allows the worshiper whose family is in turmoil because of a child's bad choices to rejoice in the Lord while petitioning him patiently for assistance that hasn't yet appeared. Faith triggers unwearied action to find solutions that no one else thinks are available, much less possible. Anguish and distress over an accident are not barriers to forward motion in the life of a woman who has a long-term faith in Christ. Loss of a job or enforced retirement don't crush the man who believes God guides his day-to-day living. As Bernard Northrup wrote, "We are to walk by faith whether we understand the trials or not!" All the stress points in life must be handled in faith, and patience comes to faith's assistance time after time.

But how does patience apply to the activity of faith, to believing God cares and blesses even if life takes u-turns and unforeseen exits? Patience takes several forms in a human character. It shows up as endurance, as a staying power, as an ability to face today's realities without complaint. When you can say, "Yes, I don't like what this situation has brought about, but I can stick with it a little longer," patience bears you up, connects with your belief in God's goodness, and summons a strength you were previously unaware you possessed but always hoped you'd have when it was needed.

"The key to everything is patience," Arnold Glasow said. "You get the chicken by hatching the egg, not by smashing it."

So it is with the application of faith in your hard times. Delay moaning over a disaster as it happens, not out of denial or anger, but because you're watching for the hand of God in the adversity. Somewhere in what you're experiencing, the Lord does a good deed, or he's about to do one. Will you delay until you see the Almighty at work? Imprudence advises you to hurry, but wisdom suggests a pause. Patience allows you to hold the horses in check and linger until the track opens up. Then God points out the hole in the pack, and the way is suddenly clear to your finish line. Now gallop! Patient faith brings home the win.

A virtuous soul needs to learn temperance, too. Especially in today's environment of runaway excitement and quick pleasures, temperance is a much maligned quality. Christian people, as well as non-religious folk, are captivated by a spirit of escapism. They desire to race their hearts and stimulate their psyches. So they engage in high risk adventure on snowy slopes, or they go alone to the sea in a small boat. People plunge themselves unrestrained into extreme pastimes like dangerous sexual activity and fearful escapades that lurk at the fringes of morality. If you wish to develop your virtuous side, you must learn temperance, but it's lessons are taught slowly. Patience is required for you to master the principles and to practice them consistently.

How can you grow in a temperate approach to life? Self-control is a starting point, but self-control isn't easy for a human being. Our species has survived a threat of extinction for millennia by stepping onto the path and openly asserting our independence of other creatures and displaying our dominance over many natural phenomena. We believe we're masters of our fate. None shall direct our movements except ourselves! Self-control is quickly misconstrued by a human as a license to pressure the world around us to serve our whims.

Truth is, we're more vulnerable than we'll admit. Often accident or *bon chance* decrees our destiny. We're not in control. As Paul explained to his co-worker Timothy,

> People will be lovers of themselves, lovers of money, boastful, proud, abusive, disobedient to their parents, ungrateful, unholy, without love, unforgiving, slanderous, without self-control, brutal, not lovers of the good, treacherous, rash, conceited, lovers of pleasure rather than lovers of God—having a form of godliness but denying its power. Have nothing to do with them.
>
> *2 Timothy 3:2-5*

Patience: Harvesting the Spirit's Fruit

From a Christian perspective, as history moves toward its completion, people will believe they're able to do whatever they please, throwing off all restraints. In other words, they'll believe they're uncontrolled by everything except private whim and flights of fancy. But, Christian, this is not possible—not for you. Because you belong to Jesus Christ, bought at the price of his life, you're called to exercise willpower. Discipline yourself in good behavior, decency, and all wholesome qualities. Strengthen your mind; understand the ways of godliness and impose upon yourself the blessings of self-control. Discover how to hold back your behavior and desires as a rider restrains the horse on which he sits. Or to put it in more modern terms, ride the motorcycle you call your life with your hand on an easy throttle. Christian, control yourself! And patience is germane to all your efforts.

In the midst of the Roaring Twenties, President Calvin Coolidge spoke before the Holy Name Society in Washington about the needs of American youth. "The worst evil that could be inflicted upon the youth of the land," he declared, "would be to leave them without restraint and completely at the mercy of their own uncontrolled inclinations. Under such conditions education would be impossible, and all orderly development intellectually or morally would be hopeless." Youth during those riotous times at the beginning of the twentieth century needed to learn self-control. Since that century has passed into the twenty-first, one wonders why so many youth and adults are still unable to discipline themselves?

Perhaps the answer lies in this: Self-restraint demands a high tax. Patience. You must walk through your days with unwearied steps. Allow a serene outlook to have sway over your mood. Trust God without complaint, listen for his Spirit's whisper with great care, and respond to the guidance of Jesus' teachings with an eagerness that develops out of long meditation. Slowly learn the ways of obedience, humility, correction and self-adjustment. God guides by inches more often than giant leaps. Observe the marks he makes on the stage floor, and hit each of the marks appointed for you on cue. He can make the drama of your life come alive only if you are a disciplined actor. Control yourself by quietly following each of his directions. Be patient until you notice how frequently you stand where you're supposed to stand and how simply you move to the place assigned for you.

As a script is the actor's major guide for his role in the play, so the Bible directs you into the storyline of human life. In its pages, God's Spirit has expressed the emotions, the virtues, the methods and the truths which will build your character. If you want to grow in patience, read what scripture says about patience and observe how biblical people are both patient and impatient. What consequences came of their endurance or lack of it? How are you able to enlist the word of God as your handbook? By thorough and patient reading, re-reading and meditation. Prayer will help, and slowly—as all exercises in patience move—you'll find your skill in this and other spiritual qualities developing one lesson after another.

In your search for a virtuous spirit, your personality has to take on finer qualities than you're accustomed to displaying naturally. Prudence is one. In the *Book of Proverbs*, wisdom is personified and tells the reader:

> "I, wisdom, dwell together with prudence;
> I possess knowledge and discretion."
>
> *Proverbs* 8:12

A virtuous person learns about life and gains discretion when she practices the ways of wisdom and prudence, which are not the same thing. As I think about prudence, I think in terms of practical wisdom. Wisdom is too esoteric, too "in the clouds."

Patience: Harvesting the Spirit's Fruit

Prudence is carefulness, caution, good sense, the opposite of recklessness. You know right from wrong; you understand that in a fallen world sin always exerts an influence even at the best moments. So you take your time before deciding on a course of action, you hesitate a moment longer, then act, and you assess how successful your activity was. Then you make adjustments if you can. Prudence enlists patience as it executes its movements. Become a careful person, and people will see virtue in your character.

Forethought doesn't always come easily. You don't see the unexpected or the accidental. So practical wisdom isn't possible in every circumstance. True, yet you can plan, analyze and regulate your response to the things you didn't anticipate. Prudence isn't a blind and blithe march into the unknown. It's a series of careful tweaks, added one upon another to an overall intention. By fine-tuning, prudence moves you ahead rather than allowing you to fall behind in life. But patience is needed. You have to learn to persevere beyond the point of surrender on some occasions. Move yourself forward by great tenacity. Alter direction ever so slightly, and the wind will pick up your sails again to carry you to your destination. Prudence is open to change and modification, but such a bendable characteristic asks for your patient progress along with confidence that God is with you, at the helm. And he studies the compass! You will not be lost on the heaving ocean.

Your quests after faith, temperance and prudence are not the only expeditions toward a virtuous soul that you make in life. Indeed, you're on multiple safaris at one and the same time, and patience has an application for each one. Virtue has a matrix of attributes. Its many distinctives rub against each other to polish and smooth one another. Fortitude and justice scrub one another clean and make your virtue shine for others to see.

How? Perhaps at work you've been subjected to harassment by an overbearing supervisor, nothing sexual, just verbal remarks that make you think either he has no social skills or he really doesn't like you or your work. With patience and virtue on your side, you can salvage—save—the situation, and your job! Knuckle down without knuckling under. Take the resilience that your faith in Jesus Christ instills, and rub kindness into the wounds the supervisor inflicts. Return appreciation for insult. That's an example of turning the other cheek, right? Become considerate toward your manager, especially when his bad side is shown again. Fortify your inner strength with the vitamins of integrity and goodwill. This means you'll have to be patient and maybe endure repetitions of rudeness. But you're suffering for righteous behavior, not sin. A virtuous soul turns distress into opportunity, abuse into compassion. By loving even your enemies, you mature into a Christian whose high caliber is acknowledged by others and can even transform adversaries into friends.

I think this is an experience similar to what Jesus referred to when he said, "Blessed are you when people insult you, persecute you and falsely say all kinds of evil against you because of me" (Mt. 5:11). You may not think you suffer as the prophets of old suffered—for the truth and righteousness of God's kingdom. But aren't you? If your supervisor presses you despite your loyal and productive service to the company, isn't the righteousness you learned from Jesus at stake? As a Christian who works for an employer, your commitment is to do high quality work for a reasonable paycheck. If an overseer is putting you down out of spite or from personal dislike, isn't he reacting to your Christian virtue? I think so. Therefore, your uncomplaining response—your patient endurance—displays kindness and generosity. It reveals that Christ's personal qualities and justice are chafing together in your life, making you a bit more like your Savior. Such virtue reveals his ability to make a good person out of an otherwise sinful one. You're a person of noble and good heart, and by perseverance you produce a good crop. Seeds of grace have taken root in your inner being to create a witness of integrity and patience that will outlast the years you work for the distressing manager. Your patience will not be lost, because it will harvest the Spirit's fruit. Your enduring witness is garnered from a virtuous soul, one that your co-workers will remember long after your retirement, one that God will reward for eternity.

Chapter Six

Impatience

To his friend Zophar, Job said,
"Is my complaint directed to man?
     Why should I not be impatient?"

Job 21:4

ARE you a traveler? If you are, then you know that a major factor in a journey is frustration. There are always delays and detours, lines to wait in, and misconnections to work around. Because this is the nature of travel, impatience easily and quickly becomes part of the tour. Try as you might to be patient, someone at sometime does something that sets off the alarm and awakens the beast in you. Because I love to go places, see new things, pass through new areas, and meet new people, I know impatience can be a problem.

As I travel, I prefer to wander as much as possible. I don't enjoy driving interstates, so when I have the time, I get off those well-beaten paths ASAP! During the afternoon on the day I write this, I journeyed 250 miles from my home for a Bible Society's annual meeting. I mapped out my route to take the

Patience: Harvesting the Spirit's Fruit

Pennsylvania turnpike to Ohio and get off at the second exit on the Ohio pike. My intent was to drop south to US 30 and head west to the conference center. I'd have the evening free to take pictures of the sunset over Pleasant Hill Lake at Mohican State Park. When I returned to the lodge, I could write for a couple of hours. Since you're reading this, you know I made it.

But not without displaying impatience!

You see, I was talking to my wife on the cell phone. Yeah, I know I shouldn't do that while driving! But I was, and as you guessed, I missed the exit. Since this was a restricted access road, I had to trek onward to the next exit—15 miles! Annoyance! I was annoyed with myself, since I had nobody else I could blame! This exit presented me with a choice I didn't want to make. I didn't want to go I-80 West. Nor did I wish to drive through Akron. (My mother used to live there, and I learned thirty-five years ago to avoid Akron traffic like the plague!) So I decided to take the first exit after the split-off from the turnpike and work my way south to Route 30. Yep, wrong move! And the wrong time of day! Aggravation!

This is when the impatience started. I found myself on the lower edge of suburban Youngstown while the schools were letting out. Traffic crawled. Lights took forever. Good thing I'm not superstitious. Within fifteen minutes, I was the *thirteenth* car behind a school bus on a two lane county road with stops every third or fourth farmhouse. More frustration. Finally, after five miles, the bus turned off! Praise the Lord! Oh, and look! Eight cars ahead of me turned left and right, too. God's common grace is wonderful! But two miles further, and the remaining southbound drivers in my shorten line found ourselves behind a truck hauling stones. By the time I was the only driver left behind the truck, I noticed three things. The tarp on the back of the stone truck had these words emblazoned on it, in red: HAVE

A NICE DAY! Yeah…right! Then I noticed the truck was going straight, and I could get on US 30 by turning right! Hallelujah! My elation was short-lived. I noticed the third thing. A delivery vehicle, a kind that's notoriously slow-moving, crossed the street in front of me, going uphill on Route 30. Disappointment!

At this junction in the road, I began to notice the telltale signs of impatience again, the ones my wife always spots seconds before I see them. I'd been calling slow-turning male drivers, *Clyde!* Audibly. With nuisance in my voice. Women drivers who did something I didn't like got the epithet, *Claudia!* The really bad ones, of either gender, received a simple, *Clown!* Of course, this rude vocal behavior is always kept inside my vehicle. Only my family who are passengers ever hear it, and I was alone today. But impatience came to my notice as I turned onto the new highway that would bring me here to the Bible Society meeting.

Then it struck me. You're a Christian preacher and pastor. You're on the way to a Bible-related meeting. You're writing a book about patience! And you don't have any right now!

Why have I gone on at such length about this? So that you'll understand better the nature of impatience and patience. And so that I will, too! These two attitudes push and pull at each other, sometimes in a creative tension, sometimes coming to blows with one another. A question raised by impatience concerns whether your behavior is right or wrong, useful or useless. Impatience can do amazing and world-shifting deeds, and it can destroy you or the people around you.

Inventors come up with new solutions to old problems when they grow impatient with the established ways of dealing with a difficulty. For instance, there's the problem of keeping shoes on your feet. We're so used to laces and Velcro and slip-ons that we forget people used to *button* their shoes. They bent over, used a small metal rod with a hook on its end, worked it through button holes in the leather, grabbed a button on the inner edge of the tongue, and yanked it through the hole! No wonder a frustrated and impatient inventor suggested poking small holes in the shoe and passing string through them, followed by tying a bow! The whole affair went from complication to simplicity.

There are other good uses for impatience. The American Revolution occurred after colonists grew intolerant enough with British governmental mistakes and abuses to rise up and shout, "No more! We will rule our own fortunes!"

New, heartier plants have been developed by agriculturalists because farmers were aggravated about poorly producing seeds and nuts, and because grocers were anxious for food that was easier to ship and handle.

People who were headed toward different careers have ended up in medical research because a loved one became ill, and their eagerness for a cure inspired them to investigate new medicine or surgical procedures.

When impatience motivates useful or creative activity, can we call it a bad human characteristic?

Still, as we all know, impatience isn't always positive. Many times, it's a huge problem. Take the difficulty we call "burn out." Disturbance, exasperation, unhappiness and stress mount up in gigantic piles in your life until your mental, physical and spiritual states collapse. Heart attacks, murders, mid-life crises, along with a myriad of other undesirable effects come from this overloaded condition. Whenever you recognize burn out in your experience, what were the signs you should have noticed earlier? Anger? Dissatisfaction? Annoyance? Depression? Impatience? Probably all of them along with additional unsettled moods. People were probably complaining that you weren't as tolerant as usual. A friend may have suggested a day off, maybe had even invited you to go fishing or shopping. Neighbors avoided you or dismissed themselves as quickly as they could. Your sons might have been embarrassed to invite buddies to the house, or perhaps their longer and longer absences in the evening had an explanation in *your* attitude. I'll bet impatience with them was top on the list, too. It can be as destructive as it is productive.

What are you to do about it? As with most human problems, admitting you're fault is a starting point. Look at how impulsive you've become, like me muttering about *Clydes* and *Claudias* in the car. Inspect the hurry-hurry lifestyle you've created. A forceful source of impatience in contemporary life is the rushing schedule we keep every day. When were you hasty, jumping into a new project before it was the right time to start? Here's an indication of impetuous behavior, which is a sign of impending exhaustion and of overwhelming stress. See your problem with impatience, then you can initiate an improvement in your character. If you don't admit you've sinned, how can anyone forgive you? how can you forgive yourself?

As we discover ourselves acting impatiently, we're able to take a breather, clear our heads, and turn our enthusiasm for confrontation into an exuberance for being a support to others. You cannot love your neighbor when you're self-absorbed. An impatient person doesn't have time for friends and neighbors, even for family! He's too narcissistic to notice what his conduct creates on the block where he lives. In order to focus on acts of compassion or encouragement, you have to be aware of the hardship and destitution others face; then your heart can extend itself beyond your own privations. To spotlight what others are going through, you have to withdraw from your own struggles, and this is where quietude and meditation come into play. As you engage in regular times of thought, prayer, and reflection, your woes lessen, your soul relaxes in faithful confidence in the arms of Christ. Then you start seeing with his eyes, feeling his emotions for the folks who people your days. The electric current of impatience can be redirected by the conduit of spiritual discipline.

A Medieval story about the apostle John tells of him standing in a woods, petting a partridge. Both he and the bird are calm in one another's presence. Then a hunter appears. He's surprised to find the great man acting so benign toward the partridge, which was often the hunter's quarry. He asked John, "Why do you treat the animal so gently?"

John's answer was succinct. "The mind needs to be soothed if it is to be effective in the Lord's work."

As you allow the stress and bother of daily living to burden your soul, you grow anxious. You worry. You're distracted from the meaning of what you do and fail to discern its impact on others. Their annoyance heightens your impulsive reactions, and when you're unguarded, you become rash, hotheaded. The excitement you create isn't positive. You want to apologize and start again, but the hasty deed has stirred up another's anger. She returns in kind what she received, and the race to separation and estrangement is on. Divorce follows a series of impatient and imprudent encounters. Confidence in a friend's good will might also dwindle into a trickle and dry up like a desert wadi. Or another church member is lost to the inactive list, or if you're lucky, he merely sits on the other side of the sanctuary. Relationships are ruined by stress-induced impatience.

However, you can do something about it—preemptively. Get into the habit of daily self-examination. Spend time in the word of God, perusing the Bible to discover the Lord's take on the human condition and its potential for good and bad conduct. Allow yourself silent moments to reflect on what you've been laboring to accomplish with all your feverish activity. Measure yourself against the revealed will of God. Have you come up short? Have you matched his expectations? Repent if needed, rejoice when able, and always review the present contents of your heart and mind. By devotional exercise, you'll cut impatience off when it's a sapling before its harmful shoots spring up all across the forest of your life. Impatience can be chased away by clear thinking and dedicated emotions, as if you're waving away an unwanted creature by brandishing a lantern in the night.

But what if your impatience aims at the relationship you have with God? You've been angry with him before. You've felt neglected by him. You've been in a hurry about finding the solution to your difficulties, and he's been silent…too long quiet in the face of your woes! Impatience with the Almighty, who appears to be the Uncaring One, has caused many humans to forsake him and to give up religion and ethics and happiness altogether. What happens when impatience steals away your fellowship with Jesus Christ?

In the Bible, perhaps Job out of all the people described on its pages had a right to be ticked with the Almighty. Satan received permission to test Job. He could do anything he wished except kill God's servant. This devilish persecution would show Job's loyalty and righteousness. The bet was on! The Adversary destroyed, one after another, Job's possessions, prosperity, and progeny. He lost all he had except his complaining wife and three well-meaning friends who weren't much help. It's little wonder Job answered his friend Zophar by saying,

> "Is my complaint directed to man?
> Why should I not be impatient?"
>
> *Job 21:4*

The righteous sufferer was impatient with God because he had not deserved such unbearable punishment as he was enduring. Sitting in sackcloth, covered with the ashes of remorse, Job was a picture of an anguished soul, cut off from all living joys and isolated even from the Lord whose fellowship he used to relish. Why shouldn't he be impatient with the Lord?

Anguished Job then launched himself into an impatient tirade against the wicked who seem not to suffer much, but rather prosper well in life. As he told Zophar,

> "Why do the wicked live on,
>   growing old and increasing in power?
> They see their children established around them,
>   their offspring before their eyes.
> Their homes are safe and free from fear;
>   the rod of God is not upon them.
> Their bulls never fail to breed;
>   their cows calve and do not miscarry.
> They send forth their children as a flock;
>   their little ones dance about.
> They sing to the music of tambourine and harp;
>   they make merry to the sound of the flute.
> They spend their years in prosperity
>   and go down to the grave in peace.
> Yet they say to God, 'Leave us alone!
>   We have no desire to know your ways.
> Who is the Almighty, that we should serve him?
>   What would we gain by praying to him?'
> But their prosperity is not in their own hands,
>   so I stand aloof from the counsel of the wicked."
>
> Job 21:7-16

Job rejected Zophar's counsel because he understood that the abundance of possessions, prosperity and progeny that the wicked might relish at the moment were not guaranteed. They might be subjected to loss by God's hand at any moment, as he had experienced. Job had a negative view of God, soured by his recent losses, but he had not forsaken the Lord. He was not like the wicked he described who bulked at the thought of serving the Almighty. He was ready to serve God at any moment despite his suffering. The patience of Job portrays a faith and a commitment that inspire those who study his character.

As the world around you multiplies reasons for you to crab and grouch and become impatient or complacent, you're being called to an opportunity. While you wonder why the disturbing people you observe are able to add treasure and power to themselves, while you can't put together a decent day of happiness, stop to consider Jesus Christ's call to you. He motions for you to walk beside him on the bitter trail, to reveal in your conduct how grace sustains the humble, how mercy lifts up the trusting, how comfort soothes the patient one. Jesus' ministry was, and is, about turning the world's pessimism inside out. He labored, endured, suffered, agonized, died and rose again in order to point the way to a lifestyle that amasses both treasure in heaven and spiritual abundance on earth. And sometimes the experience of impatience becomes part of the journey Jesus asks that you make.

Do the world's malicious people make you impatient for justice? Do foul and nasty folks impel you to extend a blessing to those who are persecuted as well as to those who persecute? What can you do? Become annoyed about people who hunger, then take up the fish and bread Christ supplies and feed a stranger. Practice Jesus' brand of peace-creating deeds for your friends. Impatience can be good. It might produce pain, but it also leads to a better world. What kind of patience do you wrestle to fashion? For the moment, it may not be an earth-redeeming patience, but only the staying power that will get you through your journey.

After I spied my own impatient attitude while on the way to the Bible Society meeting, I confessed its detrimental effects. I turned my eyes toward the landscape, my heart toward the early spring farmsteads I passed, and my mind to prayer for drivers with whom I shared the road. The old Ohio architecture I knew as a youth started to present itself to my eyes, some of it dilapidating into decay and some of it showing how much the farmers love it. Almost by accident, I located a restaurant I visited more than twenty years ago, still in business and well kept. The Amish-style food I remembered is still being served. Imagine that! As I finished my evening meal, I looked out a window and watched the Ohio I loved as a boy. Across the way, a well-painted barn graced a rural family's yard above their glassy blue pond. A mixed flock of ducks, geese and turkey wandered calmly between barn and pond. A homelike peace settled over me, along with sufficient patience to make me relax over another coffee and a piece of the best peach pie I've had in years!

Why not seek Christ's help every day to turn your annoyance into patience?

Chapter Seven

A Peculiar Patience

What strength do I have, that I should still hope?
What prospects, that I should be patient?

Job 6:11

YOU'VE asked people to pray for you, surely. A tragedy, an unexpected turn of events, a period of chaos in your usually routine life caused you to seek the intercession of others for your good. At least, you didn't turn down someone's proposal to pray, did you?

Being prayed for is a peculiar experience. Some people fear it. A skeptical man responded to my offer of prayer: "It can't hurt anything." A non-member for whom my church was asked to pray called me to request that her name be removed from our congregation's prayer list because she considered it an invasion of privacy! An odd request, I thought. But we granted it quickly. Everybody else I've known is anxious for prayers to be said for him or her. They're willing to petition God for others' blessing, too. At least they *say* they'll pray, and that's enough for me to believe they will. Yet praying raises mixed feelings in some folks.

Patience: Harvesting the Spirit's Fruit

When we pray in church, the entreaties may be printed in the bulletin or projected on a screen. They're written words of some sort. Not every request is in letters for all to read. Some are spoken words, and we offer our personal consent to the requests by saying, "Amen" when the speaker stops. I'd guess that few people leave worship without making a silent prayer for the blessing of a child or spouse or friend. Praying is both a corporate and an individual Christian experience, and each of us has a private way of speaking to God. We use a comfortable vocabulary, a posture we learned to be "correct," or we pray with an abnormal tone in our voices. Every Christian develops his or her own conversational style before God's throne of grace. Part of it is learned in Sunday school or worship, part is learned at home, and part becomes eccentrically our personal manner with the Father over the decades of our association with his Son Jesus and the Holy Spirit. Prayer is a peculiar experience, as unique and curious as each individual on the planet.

Patience belongs on the list of peculiar things, too. It's an individualized experience. Nobody else can be patient for you. Only you can be patient for yourself. Also, patience must be exercised within a particular context—*your* context. People who share the same circumstances may not be called upon by God to exercise the patience you're summoned to display nor in the manner you must be patient. Forbearance is a quality that becomes distinctive because only you are *you* in Christ. I'm *me* in Christ, and that can never be exactly the same thing as you in him. Neither can your patience be my patience. The expression of our tolerance and long-suffering will take different forms, even when we're in the same situation together. This is a curious and irregular aspect of the human display of patience.

A profound difference exists between the patience of a Christian and the quietude of a person who wants nothing to do with Jesus Christ. Any human being can be patient. Indeed, each of us must be patient at one time or another, but how we practice the virtue can't be photocopied. The non-believer may maintain a gentle, tolerant attitude out of a desire to be a likable person. A Christian might do the same. So the difference doesn't lie in the character of patience itself. It rests inside the one who practices patience. The interior dynamics of a person either cloak or disclose patience as he achieves it. Kindness and greed each employ patience but for opposing ends. What you admire and what you despise determines how patience plays out in your current situation.

A non-Christian is perhaps patient because he believes virtue is noble or useful or expected. It might be part of the mores of his culture. In order to survive in his society, he must display a restrained, long-suffering lifestyle. Maybe people he respects believe patience is a worthy quality to exhibit. Therefore, he emulates their persistence, adding his own twists on how it's expressed, but still retracing the image of other's patience, as much as possible. Serenity of face and heart may reveal the serenity in his soul. A lack of weariness when harassed may be the evidence of a genuinely patient attitude. His heart could be one that blusters easily, brags about accomplishments, and his patience displays itself in the endurance of practical jokes or snide remarks. His staying power may be motivated by revenge or self-justification. Perhaps a desire for success can create patience, as Napoleon Hill wrote, "Patience, persistence and perspiration make an unbeatable combination for success." Many things—positive or negative—can attach themselves to the practice of patience in a non-believer, but in the end his fortitude is aimed at self-preservation.

A Christian, on the other hand, desires to be patient because it was a virtue of Jesus Christ. Her Lord demonstrated patience as a highly desired trait, and therefore, she endeavors to be uncomplaining as he was uncomplaining, or to endure insult as he endured insult. The root motivation for the Christian is to become like Jesus Christ, to show the world how the Savior saves, how he brings about an abundant life. An attitude similar to the non-Christian's patience may appear in the conduct of a follower of Jesus, but the motivation is not self-preservation. The Christian isn't trying to say, "See how I've become a good and noble person!" Rather her desire is to declare, "See how wonderful my Lord is!" The motive reveals Jesus the Redeemer to the watching world. Christian patience seeks to make its Master known.

Christian patience is peculiar in another respect. It's different from a non-believer's patience at its *source*. A person who seeks to live without a regard for Jesus Christ becomes patient because of others' expectation, training, or inspiration. A disciple of Christ receives patience as a *gift*. Patience is part of the Holy Spirit's fruit within a believer's life. The source of patience within a Christian is the Spirit of the patient God who lives within his or her heart. You and I may aid the Spirit as he educates us. We do so by becoming good pupils, but the headwaters for our patience flow from a divine source.

You may feel you have a patient soul because your parents and grandparents knew how to be patient and inculcated this virtue within you. To some extent this is true. Christian patience is a learned virtue. It's learned at home as children, in church and Sunday school, from sermons and Bible studies, or through service within your congregation's committees and governing boards. Other Christians are examples for you to follow. Yet all of these experiences and mentors are merely the *mechanisms* used by God's Spirit as he teaches you patience. It's the Spirit himself who's the source of your patient attitude.

Your tolerant habits are his gift to you. Praise be to your Teacher!

In the end, each disciple and every atheist follows a pattern, an example that suggests what the content of a patient life should be. On the surface, the difference does not appear to be great. But their goals for being patient are different. Consider this: Christians and non-Christians both maintain other qualities within their characters that interact with their private expressions of patience and affect both its style and its righteousness. The distinctives of their interior lives push and pull at their patience and cause it to take on a similar appearance—the virtue in each one is identifiable as patience. Yet the endurance of the believer and the non-believer is somewhat eccentric, atypical, specialized, peculiar to the individual. Patience in a non-Christian seeks self-enhancement, while a Christian's patience seeks to glorify Christ Jesus, the patient Lord of all creation. From the world's point of view, the Christian use of patience is peculiar, and from the Christian point of view the world's use of patience is odd. Each thinks the other doesn't measure up.

The American culture at large is impatient. We desire quick approval of a bank loan. We buy our theater tickets online to save us time, but the truth is, we don't want to wait in the long line that accompanies the first few showings of a blockbuster movie. We use drive up windows at banks, restaurants, and even mortuaries! Americans are in a hurry and don't like to be delayed. We're an impatient people. As Paul Sweeney asked, "How can a society that exists on instant mashed potatoes, packaged cake mixes, frozen dinners, and instant cameras teach patience to its young?" Normal human patience is short-lived and self-centered, and stereotypical Americans are primary examples of the trait. But short-lived patience is worldly, and it's to be avoided by Christians. We're called by a divine voice to be patient in all things. The apostle Paul would advise us to do what he encouraged the Colossians to do: "...as God's chosen people, holy and dearly loved, clothe yourselves with compassion, kindness, humility, gentleness and patience" (Col. 3:12). Christians are to display virtues that go beyond the good practiced by worldly folks.

Writing in *The Imitation of Christ*, Thomas à Kempis, spoke about a believer's security in this life: "Dispose [i. e., organize] yourself...not for much rest but for great patience. Seek true peace, not on earth but in heaven; not in men or in other creatures but in God alone. For love of God, you should undergo all things cheerfully, all labors and sorrows, temptations and trials, anxieties, weaknesses, necessities, injuries, slanders, rebukes, humiliations, confusions, corrections, and contempt. For these are helps to virtue. These are the trials of Christ's recruit." In other words, patience gets exercised well by all the experiences à Kempis listed.

The genuine practice of Christian patience comes from a desire to please the Lord and live in a godly fashion despite the pummeling life dishes out. As Jesus accepted labors and anxieties, injuries and contempt, so his followers accept the need to endure their anxieties patiently. Throughout the earliest days of Christian history, you discover example after example of the peculiar nature of Christlike patience in the apostles.

For instance, the apostle Paul was called upon by the Lord to exercise patience with the churches he established in various cities. In a letter to the Thessalonian believers, Paul's serenity was obvious as he taught them about matters that confused them. Also, his lack of complaint toward the Philippians shined through in his praises for how supportive they were regarding his ministry, yet he had to ask them to amend their lives by following his example of faithful service to Christ. Then he warned them patiently...

> For, as I have often told you before and now say again even with tears, many live as enemies of the cross of Christ. Their destiny is destruction, their god is their stomach, and their glory is in their shame. Their mind is on earthly things.
>
> *Philippians* 3:18-19

As a spiritual father and tolerant teacher, Paul sought to win the Philippians to realistic Christian living in a gentle yet stern manner. Then on another occasion, he almost lost his patience with the Corinthians. That congregation's divisive nature and its resistance to Paul's guidance frustrated him during his absence from its fellowship. In his second letter to them, he listed the harsh experiences he had during his service to Christ and to the churches, things like imprisonment and sleepless nights, beatings and poverty. He enumerated the qualities of his personal character, such as "purity, understanding, patience and kindness" (cf. 2 Cor. 6:6). In exasperation, he cajoled them:

> We have spoken freely to you, Corinthians, and opened wide our hearts to you. We are not withholding our affection from you, but you are withholding yours from us.
>
> *2 Corinthians* 6:11-12

Paul was patiently pleading for reconciliation with the church. The varying circumstances and characters of each of Paul's congregations required him to show patience to the people in differing ways. In each demonstration of his tolerance, Paul revealed another side of his own patience. He could be serene, uncomplaining, strong-willed or persistent because the Spirit made him a patient apostle. The source of his patience was the Holy Spirit within him.

Patience: Harvesting the Spirit's Fruit

Being patient also changes with your circumstances. Its basic character remains intact, but its expression shifts and adapts as you struggle against anything that provokes. Unless a friend annoys you with his belching, you have no reason to suffer through it or to tell the friend how much his impoliteness bothers you. When the same pal is with you again and insists on cracking his knuckles over and over, you have another occasion to turn annoyance into a patient explanation of better manners. On his next visit, as you listen to a favorite album and he taps on your table with a pencil from his pocket, your vexation is a third motivation for patience—provided you still what this oddball as a friend! As conditions alter over the time of your association, friendship paints patience with different colors—kindness, generosity, compassion, whichever is most necessary at a given moment.

Patience is peculiar. It cannot be expressed without having an abrasive stimulus. It requires something to rub at it, to make it raw until it must raise up an arm, point a finger to the sky, and say, "How can this be made better? How can I end the irritation?" A patient person must be chafed in order to retaliate, not with anger or vengeance, but with tolerance, serenity or fortitude. The apostle tells us, "Love is patient." No wonder! Love isn't self-seeking, nor is it quickly infuriated. It doesn't harm or suspect. When irritated, love perseveres. In short, it *is* patient. Our relationships with other people demand qualities like confidence, long-suffering and persistence, but living closely with someone exposes you to rashness, misplaced enthusiasm, impulsiveness, edginess, as well as other interpersonal problems. Patience must rise up when scratched without scratching back. Catfights are not a product of patience!

This brings us back to the content of a human heart and mind. Impure thoughts about another person makes a man impatient with himself, perhaps with his spouse. Jealousy of a friend's success can make a kind woman into an anxious ogre. Drunkenness causes parents to lose patience with children, and sometimes the reverse happens. Children become exasperated with the old man! Dissent between neighbors leads to ill feelings that last until one of them moves. The content of your heart and mine affects your patience. If sins have control, you're less likely to try to be silent and long-suffering. You lash out for some sort of pay back or self-justification. You develop an eagerness to be proven right in all your opinions and regarding your knowledge or expertise. In short, sin uses your impatience to make you unfit to live with another.

The content of the heart determines the volume of the patience that sings out of it. Allow gentleness and forgiveness to infiltrate your thinking, and patience speaks from the center of your actions toward family and friends, strangers, too. Hunger for righteousness, and patience floods into the corners of your character ready to be expressed in a moment, without hesitation. Plan to be a merciful person, as Jesus Christ was merciful, and you become known as a soft-spoken, quiet, caring man or woman. People will assume you're patient. Whatever you store up in your heart becomes the treasure that enriches your staying power in an overbearing world, or it becomes the rusty bucket out of which you cannot pour even a drop of patience for any other thirsty soul.

Patience is peculiar. Your son who has learned from you how to be merciful will not resonate patience with quite the same tones as you do. He'll find a way to be merciful and tolerant in an idiom that suits his soul's song. Your spouse won't squeeze out a patience to match yours, although it also begins from a forgiving attitude. A neighbor from the same block, who attends the church you attend and listens to the sermons you hear, will use the preacher's lessons about sobriety and happiness to demonstrate patience in a way you'd never imagine. Patience is an individualized quality, although it may be inspired by the same Holy Spirit in a heart much like your own.

Look at Job's experience in the Old Testament. The trial of Job's patience was only beginning. With a sore faith in God, a faith bruised by the assaults of his tormentor, Job despaired. He told a friend,

> "Oh, that I might have my request,
> that God would grant what I hope for,
> that God would be willing to crush me,
> to let loose his hand and cut me off!
> Then I would still have this consolation—
> my joy in unrelenting pain—
> that I had not denied the words of the Holy One."
>
> *Job 6:8-10*

Job was willing for God to forsake or destroy him, but he'd cling to one certainty in his heart—he hadn't forsaken God. Rather, Job had lived according to the revealed thoughts of the Holy One, his teachings, his words. This is the form of Job's peculiar patience. He knew he'd been righteous and faithful to the Almighty; therefore, his relentless anguish wouldn't eclipse his confidence. Although at times he didn't sound so convinced, Job dared to move forward, tentatively, yes, but still forward.

As he assessed the life he'd been handed, he was ready to complain. The complaint came out in the form of two questions. He asked his friend Eliphaz the Temanite,

> What strength do I have, that I should still hope?
> What prospects, that I should be patient?
>
> *Job 6:11*

He'd lost his children, his crops and herds, his wealth and all the things people consider good blessings from heaven. He felt as if

78

he had no vigor to move ahead in life. How could he hope for anything better? He had no prospects, no assurance that all would turn around. Nothing seemed to be in his favor. Why should he be patient? Yet the anxious emotions Job expressed in his questions demonstrated the presence of his idiosyncratic patience, a longsuffering that grew out of his private experience with God—which his visiting friend had so much trouble understanding.

When you're grieved and depressed, you'll vacillate between confidence and fear. Your sadness may be a prelude to a sudden push forward as hopeful hands reach upward and a shaking voice expresses the desire to hear divine words and truth. The waiting, the pushing, the shaking, the voicing of complaint are each an aspect of your long-lasting faith in the Lord Jesus. For Christian friends who want to comfort you but don't know how patience could survive in your troubled heart, your actions are clear indications of faith and endurance. But people who don't believe Christ cares enough to listen to their complaints and woes will never be patient enough to endure the agony of a soul like yours that looks for Jesus' answers to life's miseries.

Is your life currently in a shamble? Are you waddling and shuffling through the days, wondering why tragedy or accident plague you? Are you losing patience? Complaint may be on the tip of your tongue every time you go to worship. Your church friends may sense the struggle in your soul, and you may have explained to a few trusted Bible study companions how weary you are of the spiritual wrestling match. You may find the unusual station you occupy at this moment is an enlarging burden, and you may not have much assurance that people understand your mood.

Your life, on the other hand, may be filled with the joy of accomplishment and the satisfaction of prosperous days. You've been making headway at work, at home, among family and friends, or business associates. Your burdens are the stresses of success. Impatience urges you to work hard, move faster, forget rest and quietness, to neglect worship and the study of scripture. Life has a good, sharp edge on it, yet you're frustrated by the temptation to be less attentive to your heart and mind, to your relationship with Christ. Let the creative juices run! Gain treasures and acquire pleasures! You deserve the rewards of a productive life. If this is your happy lot, if your horizons are bright, beware! You stand at a peculiar fork in the road of faith-building, and patience is more necessary than ever!

Remember that God your heavenly Father leads you through whatever circumstances populate your experience each day, or he allows you to create your own messes out of which you must work with his help. Persist! Persevere! Wait upon the Lord! By the fortitude provided from faith in Christ, and by trust in his Spirit, you're being led toward a curious peace that surpasses understanding. Patience is required from you regardless of whether you saunter through a flowering meadow or slog through a snake-infested swamp. How you express this patience will be peculiar to you, molded by your own eccentric walk with the Savior day by day.

Chapter Eight

Patience Incarnate

Bear with each other and forgive whatever grievances you may have against one another. Forgive as the Lord forgave you.

Colossians 3:13

WHERE have you observed patience? Rummage through your childhood memories. Perhaps you first detected patience in a grandparent. Your grandfather was always ready to explain a mysterious thing to you, how a radio worked or what made the sky blue and the grass green. He was a quick, witty and thorough teacher. From him you learned the discipline of waiting for a fish to move the bobber on your line, followed by the exhilaration of the strike and set as you began to move the fish toward you. Someone in your early years was patient with you. Who was it? How has he or she incarnated patience for you?

All virtues must be learned by discovering them in another person. You can read every book you find regarding a virtue like patience. Go to libraries, used book stores, the chain stores at a mall or to an internet site, and purchase every volume you see that has anything to do with patience. You'll never study patience as well from printed words about it as you'll learn from the imprint of practiced patience on another human being's soul. Patience must be incarnate, or it'll forever be a disembodied wish, a dream, a phantom, a wisp of smoke. Perceive it in someone you respect, and you'll discover it growing slowly in your heart, too.

Why is this so? Because we practice what our loved ones are in order to become who we'll be. I remember an anti-smoking commercial from decades ago. An adoring boy and his happy father sit under a tree, and Dad reaches for a cigarette, lights it and puffs with satisfaction. The commercial ends with a small hand above the cigarette pack now on the ground between the duo. Children learn the basics of what they become as adults from their families. Sure, they'll be changed and shaped by people outside the home, too. Peer pressure is felt throughout life, whether at school, on the job or during a softball game. Patience is learned and unlearned all the time in many contexts, but a precious resource for learning this discipline is found in the house where you lived as a child, among your earliest teachers.

To understand patience you must consider how it's also a *corporate* experience. Beyond your individualized expressions of patient behavior, your social groupings also instruct you in endurance, tolerance, and persistence. How you value this virtue will be challenged and altered, fashioned and re-fashioned by the people who surround you. And in reverse, your practice of serenity and fortitude molds their patience and impatience. The cross-fertilizing effects of private exchanges between people who care what the other person thinks caress a patient character into existence, or such exchanges abuse you into an impatience that reproduces in your children or in an elderly parent who's under your care. This virtue moves from generation to generation just as both prejudice and tolerance move. Peer groups outside the home also illustrate the corporate aspect of learning patience.

Who taught you to be annoyed when opposing politicians debate the obvious? Who explained how to become impetuous while making decisions? Who inculcated in you a zeal for extreme sports, along with the irritation that comes when your skill isn't as good as you'd like it to be? You learn impatience from the groups around you. Mothers and aunts, clergy and church members, co-workers and brothers at the lodge, teachers and students—all the important people in your days inspire you to be rash or edgy, easygoing or charitable. Impatience and patience are corporate experiences. They're learned because you see them incarnated in someone else.

The dynamics of family life are loaded with moments that require patience or instill impatience. At a clan picnic on the Fourth of July, everybody's there, and somebody gets miffed, right? A cousin teases too eagerly about your weight gain or about the whining of your toddler. Embarrassment in front of the clan makes you lash out hastily. Your impetuous words make her mother irritable, and for the remainder of the picnic, she glares at you every time you go for another soft drink. You suspect that your mother said something to your aunt, too. Why does she always step into the middle of your affairs? By the time the evening hot dogs are finished, you're ready to leave early, but your husband is too engrossed in the horseshoe match. On the way home, later, you find yourself impatient with him, too. The picnic started out well enough, but annoyance colored your family's quality time together. Your lack of patience filtered throughout the clan.

The corporate energy of patience works in a way similar to impatience, too. Your adolescent child hasn't yet learned the wisdom that hard knocks will teach him. For the moment, he knows more than you about every subject he has any interest in pursuing. He doesn't realize that your well-meaning suggestions are designed to help him avoid unnecessary trouble. After patiently expressing your opinion, you decide to let him do the unwise activity he hopes to enjoy. You summon your fortitude and trust he'll discover his mistaken notions. Serenity doesn't comfort you much on the night of the event, but when he gets back and complains about how stupid his friends were to insist that they go where they went, you patiently ride out his tirade and inject your "I told you so" comments very carefully and tactfully. Your desire is to aid his discovery of the wisdom of parental advice. Perhaps he'll also wander across your patient example, too. Now wouldn't that be a refreshing marvel? Believe me, it does happen!

The family is a basic incarnation of the patient or impatient mindset. Husbands and wives may only ever learn a grudging tolerance for one another's opinions or habits. Many a divorce occurs as a result of the inability of spouses to be truly patient with one another, and if divorce is somehow avoided and the marriage lasts decades, an agitated silence may rule the roost for days at a time. Frequently, it's one marriage partner who suffers long and patiently to keep the marriage happy enough to continue. But what does the push and pull of an impatient couple produce within their children? Do they learn good habits of endurance? Perhaps so. Perhaps not. Wouldn't a frank and caring discussion of the husband and wife's shared virtues and vices create the staying power the family needs? Maybe, yes. Maybe, no. Much depends on what each parent learned as they were growing up in their parent's homes. The impatient environment of their upbringing will greatly color the character of their home—positively, negatively, or in a mixed fashion. A couple may need to consider how well they put flesh and bones on their rehearsal of patience within the home.

The corporate responsibility for patience is enormous. It encompasses social groupings outside the family. Churches, like all other human organizations, must develop ways to incarnate patience within their mutual relationships. This is why the apostle Paul encouraged the Colossians with this advice: "Bear with each other and forgive whatever grievances you may have against one another. Forgive as the Lord forgave you" (Col. 3:13). As a congregation's members interact regarding the important matters of worship and witness, mission and spiritual maturity, they get on one another's nerves. They come to disagreements about procedures or expenditures. Differing philosophies about appropriate Christian activities become the breeding ground of intolerance, mistaken enthusiasm or anxiety about change within the congregation. Anger is expressed, or frustration is voiced. Forbearance is necessary. Grievances need to be settled amicably. Forgiveness becomes mandatory. And what is forgiveness? Forgiveness is a disciplined application of patience to the bad situation.

Throughout the Old Testament, God's patience with Israel made salvation possible for his repeatedly impatient people. Their sins took root in a desire to have their own perceptions of a good life made real, and to have that good life now. They wanted a human king and the supposed security he could bring. So they turned against their divine King, who expressed both infinite patience and annoyance with them until they learned through tough times how to trust him as their best Protector. Yet generation upon generation had to relearn the lesson. How his people always tried his patience! But God's example is always incarnated in a poet, a prophet or a sage who summons the people back to a healed relationship. The story of the Old

Testament is largely an expression of God's longsuffering and tolerance, his persistence with an edgy people.

The gospels reveal Jesus in the midst of people who fail to understand his words and deeds. Not just the Pharisees and teachers of the law, not only Roman officials and the common people of the street, but his own disciples, too! Time and time again the disciples cannot comprehend Jesus' thoughts or his activities. Shortly before his arrest, Jesus was consoling the disciples. Philip said to him, "Lord, show us the Father and that will be enough for us" (Jn. 14:8). Jesus probably took a deep breath and summoned patience as he answered his confused follower.

> "Don't you know me, Philip, even after I have been among you such a long time? Anyone who has seen me has seen the Father. How can you say, 'Show us the Father'? Don't you believe that I am in the Father, and that the Father is in me? The words I say to you are not just my own. Rather, it is the Father, living in me, who is doing his work."
>
> *John 14:9-10*

Read through any of the gospels, particularly *Mark*, and you'll discover how upsetting the disciples' misunderstandings must have been to the Lord Jesus. He had to exercise patience with them, even as he was saving them and preparing them to work in God's kingdom. Like his Father with the people of Old Testament times, Christ displayed endurance and serenity, patience unrelenting, as he blessed the Twelve.

If God, Jesus, and the apostle Paul needed to bring patience to the forefront of their dealings with the church, then is it surprising to think the incarnation of patience among today's congregations is absolutely necessary? Yet churches split because one group thinks the pastor's sermons aren't dynamic enough, or the worn carpet in the sanctuary should not be replaced at this time, or contemporary Christian songs are the only way to praise God. The body of Christ as it's revealed in any given congregation has to be attentive to the practice of patience among its members. This is a corporate fact of life, and it's more incumbent upon the church than upon all other human institutions. Congress has its own issues with patience among Senators and Representatives. Universities have to learn how to incorporate patience into their processes within a faculty and inside the classrooms and student union. But the Christian community is at the center of God's efforts to bring his surpassing peace to humanity. The church above all other organizations must exercise patience within itself.

The church's divinely appointed mission of proclaiming the gospel and evangelizing the world also places a demand for endurance and persistence squarely on its shoulders. Patience is one of the virtues that foster salvation among the world's people. When annoyance develops between church members, how well is a congregation able to proclaim salvation? Will neighbors want to unite with the church or even visit a worship service when the congregation's reputation for belligerence precedes it? The church is the pedestal on which God erects a light for all human beings to see his Son. If the light flickers because those who tend the flame argue impatiently over how to keep the light burning, or whose responsibility it is to carry the wood, then their impatience will cause the world to fall into darkness. Jesus will not be seen, and if he becomes invisible, who will look to him for help?

Here is where your personal habit of patience becomes crucial within the congregation where you serve God. As you incarnate a spirit of forbearance, other Christians will know where to turn for advice on how to stymie intolerance and annoyance between themselves and others. Your slowness to speak and eagerness to listen, tolerantly assessing and carefully drawing good inferences from the options open to the board on which you serve, will earn you a reputation for patience. People will listen for your wisdom, and they'll give it greater weight than the words of an irritable board member who spouts off about everything in a narrow-minded tone. Your patience teaches other members a virtue they will need in present and future crises—personal and corporate. Determine that you will incarnate patience as often as possible.

Beyond family life and church life, your work life requires that you learn how to be patient. Job descriptions never explain how much frustration an employee must endure, but every job has its share of nuisance and disturbance. Every dissatisfaction encountered in your workplace is an opportunity for patience. As a Christian employed to do specific tasks, you have the additional obligation of maintaining a character that honors your Lord. So you must be a leader in patience for your boss and co-workers, but they won't make your leadership easy to offer, if they don't sense how valuable a virtue patience is. Educating a non-Christian to the practice of patience will require your best spiritual energies.

This is not to hint that every office or factory, restaurant or shoe store that's operated by someone who isn't a church-goer is destined to be an environment where anxiety and intolerance rules. Many non-Christian managers and human relations people are decent folks who've learned a worldly version of patient behavior, and they make the store or warehouse a tranquil place to labor. Yet your burden as a Christian who works for a good employer remains the same. You have to lead the way in patience with clients, sales representatives, co-workers and customers. When you claim to follow Jesus of

Nazareth, people expect to see patience and other aspects of the Spirit's fruit in whatever you do.

Even businesses operated by believers are subject to hassled relationships and chaotic days. Schedules loom overhead as projects near completion. Supplies run short despite careful inventory procedures. Deliveries are delayed by the unforeseen. Each of these and a hundred other causes of stress make the most devout disciple irritable, edgy and hasty. Regardless of how careful you are, impatience at work creeps into your workforce, or the nature of your industry itself will overpower the most patient people on your staff. If you're the boss, you may need to guard yourself more closely during the rush periods for your business. Your leadership in tolerant persistence will set a tone of cooperation and collegiality that will make your enterprise flow smoothly on an ocean of swirling details.

Christian workers and managers are called by a divine voice to be the incarnation of Jesus Christ where they labor day in and day out. This is true of all the pieces of the Holy Spirit's fruit— kindness, peace, self-control and so forth. But patience is our current concern. How can you display Christ's patience to the woman in the next cubicle or the guy from the mailroom? This is a tough question to answer when the object of your patience isn't a patient person herself. Your cubicle-mate may snap when you suggest a better way to file information on her workstation. Ask yourself, "Why might she be curt so often?" Listen to her complaints at break time. Perhaps she's worried about a teenage son. Maybe she had someone dear to her die recently. She could be a proud person who considers suggestions to be a threat to her expertise. Your practice of patience must include sympathy, empathy, and genuine interest in the people you work beside. As you understand their hearts, minds and experiences better, you'll be equipped to embody Christ's longsuffering and serenity. Do this, and you fashion a work environment where tolerance flourishes and aggravation diminishes. Those around you grow more patient as you're patient with them. Patience is a corporate reality. It has to find expression wherever human beings gather in groups.

This fact makes patience a necessary commodity throughout an entire society. As I move about American culture, I discover innumerable instances of impatience. Road rage is a direct result of an impatient person colliding with another individual. Construction projects may be slipshod when completed because somebody wants to make a profit from the job and move on to another lucrative contract. Potentially top quality movies are uneven in the presentation of an important story because a producer is pressured by the money people to hold the line on costs. The result is a film with superb actors and competent directors which could have been a masterpiece now being mediocre entertainment and a box office flop. Impatience runs throughout our society. This vice is just as much a corporate experience as its opposite virtue.

As Christians in the American culture, what are we doing to raise the standard? Do we speed and weave in and out of traffic as aggressively as others? Or do we set high the bar of patience on the open road, forcing ourselves not to frustrate other travelers? Do we vote for school levies that will properly aid teachers? Or do we vote to hold the line on educational costs and thereby cause the teachers who instruct our children to limp along with dissatisfying textbooks and with computers three steps down on the technological ladder? You can greatly affect the mood of society by the way you approach its serious issues and practices. Do you tolerate a doctor who has no patience with your questions related to your elderly father's health? Or do you gently and compassionately insist, with a longsuffering patience, that she listen to what you've observed about your Dad's lack of stamina and chronic pain? Patience is a key to handling the issue of good health care on a person-to-person level. How you act, Christian, will influence your doctor's practice of medicine. Are you willing to forsake complaint and irritation over delayed medical tests in order to lead your physician's nurses to understand how nervous you are to receive the results? Patience...patience...patience is crucial as we all work toward a good society, as we pursue happiness together.

Incarnating patience is a ubiquitous need underlying many of our society's woes. Counselors who work with people addicted to drugs and alcohol need excellent skills in patience. State workers in unemployment offices hear woeful tale after woeful tale and must not allow themselves to become cynical. If they're not careful, they'll slip into intolerance and won't be helpful to people in crisis. As housing markets fluctuate, buyers and sellers, bankers and mortgage brokers, lawyers and real estate agents all border on a jumpiness that makes expensive mistakes. People in poverty become nervous about basic necessities while wasting money as a result of trying to control their own destinies to some extent. They need to learn the self-control which patience teaches. The rich and prosperous fall into traps laid by success. They have what they need and become impatient to preserve what they've gained without making a smaller profit than in the prior year. How many times have you heard it said that Company X's stock was in jeopardy because their profit margin slipped below last year's level? Lack of patience lurks somewhere behind the scenes, surely.

Christians do much for society as they put flesh and bones on the habits of patient living. The attitude of waiting to make a purchase until they have the financial means in hand will teach their children and friends the virtue of restraint in the use of credit. Patience is a foundation for such fiscal responsibility. If enough Christians are careful with the management of cash and credit, society will change. Incarnate patience with your money, and you can create a new world. Societies mature and degenerate in relation to the people who populate them.

Through Christian missions in cities throughout the United States, the virtue of patience can be, and is being, taught to people whose lives are in a shambles. I sit on the board of a men's ministry that uses private counseling, Bible study, prayer, discussion, example and other means to guide residents toward mental and spiritual maturity. Not only must the staff exercise and incarnate a deep patience, but they work toward instilling it in the men. I know about several inner city missions in Boston and Pittsburgh, which are duplicated around the country, who bring patience into their various ministries with people in our society as they struggle through self-inflicted woes. Anyone who works regularly with the afflicted knows the value of displaying patience.

To understand patience you must judge how its corporate dynamics work. Your private incarnation of patience joins your social encounters with endurance, perseverance and serenity. Your evaluation of this virtue challenges and alters you and those around you. It recasts the culture where you live, and in reverse, society's calmness or lack of it shapes your patience and impatience. How patience operates in your family, at your jobsite, within your local church, everywhere you go, relates to your own patience or lack of it.

Isn't this good motivation to harvest the Spirit's fruit?

Chapter Nine

The Artistry of Patience

Be patient...until the Lord's coming. See how the farmer waits for the land to yield its valuable crop and how patient he is for the autumn and spring rains. You too, be patient and stand firm, because the Lord's coming is near.

James 5:7-8

LOOKING at the many aspects of human living, effort and achievement, I see artistry in nearly everything we do. Art sets our species apart from the other creatures who inhabit the earth. Sure, chimpanzees, elephants and pigs have painted "pictures," but their artwork resembles abstract forms which are debatable in their expression of form, beauty, meaning and purpose. Even human abstract paintings are criticized as expressionless. Art is a distinctive trait of human nature, I think, because the love of beauty, form and meaning have been inherited by our species from the image of God which he put within us when our race was formed.

Someone sets out to sculpt a bust of a famous person. She doesn't merely begin to chip away at marble. The artist studies the individual's features, reads about the fellow's undertakings, his successes and failures. From a knowledge of the person's incongruent life and passions, she pulls together a portrait of the celebrity in her mind, a portrait that reveals truths about the object of her study. She probably sketches on paper various facets of the personality as she wishes to interpret him. The sketches are put away and brought out again, altered and refined until the artist's vision of the quarry is ready for chiseling into life from a block of stone. The result is a bust which others pronounce to be a marvelous portrayal of the luminary.

Art is the result of disciplined observance and assessment as much as it is talent and interpretation. It is also part science, part intuition and part good fortune. And I see this in so many human endeavors—those of Christians and nonbelievers alike. An entrepreneur is as much artist as business person. His dream of providing a service to others or making a product to simplify life requires his invention, inspection and interpretation. The entrepreneur must be a knowledgeable individual, a visionary, a person willing to think, to tear apart and build again, to use the unexpected occurrence to his advantage, to draw together disparate ingredients until his dream is reality. He is an artist.

Christian mothers and fathers are also artists, forging their children into a holy and good representation of God's people. Your use of humor in the home, of gentle discipline regarding bed time and relaxation time, of listening skills and prayer—all of this and more is drawn together in your creativity as you mold the clay God has given you. Your artist's eye tells you how well and how inaccurately your children are becoming depictions of Jesus Christ for others to admire and imitate, too, in the artistry of their lives. Making disciples is an art that puts a whole new spin on your parenthood. It demands the best skill and intuition you can muster.

94

The Artistry of Patience

Everywhere I turn, I see artists at work, and when I think about practicing patience, I discover yet another arena where you and I, and all God's people, must create harmony out of our thoughtful planning, our insightful vision, our care and cunning, so that a lovely portrait of patience is painted by the colors of our behavior. Patience is part science, part invention and part good fortune under the grace of God. It's an artistic expression. Rather than using pigment or clay, we employ our attitudes and opinions, our choices and activities, our relationships and commitments to craft a life that endures all things, tolerates all mistakes, works without complaint, and suffers long to create a patient personality that reflects Jesus Christ's longsuffering. To succeed as a patient person you have to become an artist.

Why?

Surely, you and I need a strong, passionate motivation in order to pursue a patient life as our witness to the soul-improving Lord we serve. An actor might ask himself, "What's my motivation? Why does the person I'm portraying in this movie do what he does? Why does he say what he says? What motivates his behavior?" The actor as artist probes for the incentives that urge his character onward in the face of crisis. He wants to understand what drives the character's enthusiasm despite the setbacks of the story's plot. What impels him forward? When the actor comprehends this, he perceives how to perform the role he has in the film. So what's the stimulus for you to become a patient person? Where is the root purpose, the spur to action, that will take you beyond a wish to be as patient as Christ and cause you to develop a truly serene heart like his? Why take up the artistry of patience in your life?

The New Testament writer James offers me a reason to practice the art of patience. He wrote, "Be patient...until the Lord's coming. See how the farmer waits for the land to yield its valuable crop and how patient he is for the autumn and spring rains. You too, be patient and stand firm, because the Lord's coming is near" (Jas. 5:7-8). How does this motivate me? In this simple way: When I became a Christian, God did not take me out of this world. He left me here and promised that Jesus would come again. He left me here, not without purpose, but for reasons that are as varied as the tapestry he weaves out of each human life. Yet patience is part of the reason I am still alive and serving him in this world. By waiting actively for Christ to return, which James says involves patience, I serve my Lord with distinction. I'm motivated to be a patient person because I want my Lord to find me acting like him when he gets back.

Now, harvesting the fruit of the Spirit—all of its seeds—kindness, generosity, patience and the like—demands my most superb efforts along with the mercy and provision of God. His wisdom is needed, but my action is also necessary. To wait idly for Jesus to fulfill his promise to return is wrong. To wait patiently, by practicing the disciplines of endurance and serenity is the right thing to do, just as loving others is right, as bringing peace to the earth is right. The fruit of the Spirit, every aspect of it, is given by the breath of God so that you and I might participate in an artful assembly of our human souls. As we learn the disciplines of patience, love and joy, we manifest the Spirit of God to a world that so desperately needs to see a reason to hope, that needs to see the coming return of Jesus as he completes the salvation of those humans who are being redeemed along with us. "...be patient and stand firm, because the Lord's coming is near..."

Here's my incentive for patience. Here's the impulse that nudges me into all the aspects of Christian living that make me, I hope, a bright testimony of my Savior's grace and goodness. I'm a brush in the Artist's hand! Or the hue he touches to the canvas here and there and here, so that the picture he's envisioned becomes a harmonious and beautiful expression of his love for humanity. My patience is one of the qualities in God's painting. It's a subtle nuance, a tint that causes someone else to say, "Oh! This picture is lovely. I must have it before the sale ends." When Jesus returns, the gavel will fall and the sale will be over. Perhaps my patient life, and yours, will have been the deciding factor in another's purchase of God's artwork.

So how do we harvest this aspect of the Spirit's fruit—patience?

Examine the tools which are at each and every Christian's disposal. Sharpen them or clean them up. Use the tools God designed for your daily application as you grow in his grace, as you tend the soil of your heart.

Begin with prayer.

If you want to become a more patient person, then talk to the Lord about your hope, and request his help in learning the habits of patience. But don't start your prayers by asking for more patience. Praise God; adore him for having created such a character trait as patience. He, after all, is the embodiment of patience par excellence. Without God's use of patience in dealing with you and me, we would have little reason to discover the ways of this virtue as we exercise it between ourselves. Since God loves us, he's patient with us, and as he expects us to love one another because he initially cared about us, so he now intends for you and me to be longsuffering and tolerant with each other. God himself is the inventor of patience. Praise him in your prayer for doing so.

Next, your prayer needs to become an admission, a confessional statement of your self-knowledge. You've been far too impatient. Admit the sinfulness of most of your impatient tirades. Acknowledge that you may have been justified at times in a few of your annoyed or impetuous episodes, but usually your impatience has been a sin. Solemnly announce in your prayer to God how serious you are about turning from a practice of unrighteous anxiety and irritation. Come clean about your need for wisdom regarding the use of patience with your children, your spouse, even regarding yourself! Divulge to the Lord how much you need the Holy Spirit's instruction.

Now you're ready to express your gratitude for the moments when you did manage to be patient with pushy co-workers or irate neighbors or fear-producing strangers. Tell God how you know it was the Spirit's presence with you when you were patient in the past. Thank him for caring enough about you and the relationships you have with other people to put a scrap patience in your soul. Thank him for the new willingness you have to grow in patience. Thank him for the promise to guide you into a holier life.

At this point in your prayer about patience, you're ready to ask for the Almighty's direct assistance in the labor of learning patience. While you ask for his help, request the names of people with whom who should become more tolerant. Fall into silence if you must, beseeching him to communicate to your heart the people with whom *he* wants you to exercise more patience. Pause with a notebook and a pen. Make out the list that comes to mind. (Don't you believe God will share such information with you? I believe he will.) Ask whatever you want, in Jesus' name, and the Father will lead you to the starting points of his response. You do serve a living God.

Your prayer about becoming a more patient Christian, a believer who's more like Jesus Christ, has not yet ended. Intercede for the people whose names came to mind as you prayed earlier. Ask God to explain more to you over the next few weeks about why and how you need to develop greater fortitude or acceptance or serenity while around each of these people. Ask him to enter into your relationship with them, to send his Holy Spirit to intercede for you with each of the individuals. Seek more love and appreciation for the better qualities in your acquaintances.

I know. This kind of prayer sounds time-consuming. Well, it is, but you want to learn patience, don't you? Harvesting the Spirit's fruit takes time. Remember James' farmer. Farmers have to wait and wait. Harvesting the Spirit's fruit also demands your commitment and, how else can I say it? Your patience. So persist in your prayers about this virtue. Repeat them as necessary. And remember: prayer about patience—conversing with your Lord about this discipline—is only the *beginning* of his instruction. More steps follow.

Scripture reading, for instance. The Bible is the guidebook for Christian conduct. Dig into it. Use a concordance or a software program to look up references to patience in the word of God. Read them. (An appendix at the back of this book lists a few such references to get you started.) Become familiar with what God's people have learned and recorded in the past for your edification. Scripture is full of teachings about patience from many perspectives. Allow the Holy Spirit, whose fruit you're harvesting, the privilege of instructing you with God's own testimony about patient behavior.

While you struggle with being patient in the weeks ahead, come back to the Bible for inspiration, comfort, advice and correction. You're repetitive reading of scripture will chastise and change you. Insights will fall over one another as you apply the lessons of God's word to your actual practice of endurance and longsuffering. It'll be as if God is layering your heart and mind with thin sheets of metal (patience) and hammering a new design on your personality. Like a sculptor in metal, he'll be polishing your new exterior, and you'll glisten with serenity and persistence. The remodeling will go deeper into your soul, too. God will shake loose the old rafters of intolerance and impulsiveness. From the inside out, the Bible will reconstruct you. As the *Letter to the Hebrews* puts it, "...the word of God is living and active. Sharper than any double-edged sword, it penetrates even to dividing soul and spirit, joints and marrow; it judges the thoughts and attitudes of the heart" (Heb. 4:12). Such scripture study may be painful, but it is also necessary and therapeutic. Yet there's a reward for your endurance in it. People will begin to see you as a more patient person than they remembered you to be in months past. Such is the joy of earnest Bible study.

Another helpful tool you might want to try is journaling. Keep a diary while you develop the spiritual discipline of patient living. Use the art of writing to your advantage. A good place to journal is your laptop computer. You can put a password on the word processor file you use for the notebook. In this way your musing about patience, about your successes and failures, will be truly confidential. However, a standard paper diary can also be private. While you write in your journal, include by all means thoughts about the fiascos, the breakdowns, the bankruptcies of your patience. Failure is the best teacher. As you re-read the record of your missteps on the journey toward greater patience, you'll discover new insights and avoid the old habits that skulk behind zeal to misdirect it. Your thinking about patience will become clearer, and your genuine growth will be confirmed over and over. The journal will be a running conversation with yourself, perhaps even God. It's strange yet comforting how writing a journal can become prayer in black and white.

You also need conversations of another type. Speak with Christians you know about patience. Enlist their advice along your path to this virtue. They've made the trip, too. They'll help you find patience more quickly in stressful situations, and they'll hold you accountable, too. It's easy to be lenient with yourself when you fall into an impatient attitude with somebody, but a Christian friend will point out how you ought to have reacted to the irritating person. Think about her advice, and you'll expand your awareness of patience as well as your application of it.

If you're part of a small group Bible study or discussion fellowship, don't hesitate to bring up the subjects of patience and impatience during the group's free time, or when it occurs in the scripture under consideration. Don't do it too often, but when you need serious guidance, ask for it. You'll be excited by the stimulus of other believers' struggles with the same problem or ambition. The exchange of spiritual lessons learned will guide your thinking and ease your uncertainties.

Another Christian you should consult is your pastor or counselor. These professionals have worked with many people in all sorts of venues. Their suggestions and insights will be invaluable. It helps to know that your pastor is praying for your success in mastering the disciplines of patience. He or she will also help to keep you accountable by asking how the effort to learn is going. When you speak to your trusted spiritual guide, solicit proposals about how to handle the trouble spots you're encountering with anxious relationships. Patience grows when carefully tended by the seasoned farmer you're becoming, so be sure to share your triumphs, too.

Worship and the sacraments are additional tools that God gives you for growth in the grace of patience. As you forget to fidget during a long hymn or sermon, you'll discover what patience can bring in the way of spiritual lessons. Beyond this, God will use both the liturgy of your congregation and the observance of the Lord's Supper to sooth your frustrations over impatience. These are Jesus' established means of grace which he designed to become tools for spiritual development. By praising him for the patience you feel widening within you, you'll receive greater motivation for the disciplined use of patience in your daily life. Regular use of worship and the sacraments reveals God's patience as he nurtures his people.

Also, don't neglect the making of a personal plan for your growth in patience. Set goals. Create a map for your journey, perhaps writing it down in your journal. From time to time, evaluate your progress toward the goals you adopted, but be prepared to redraw the trail markings and the roadblocks on your map. Detours are encountered, yet that's part of the fun in maturing spiritually. Be assured that having a personal plan to become increasingly more patient is a strong influence on the improvement of your character. You'll see how you're becoming more like Jesus Christ, who's the most patient person you'll ever meet, who's your prime example.

The artistry of patience is visible in proportion to your use of the tools of Christian growth. Combine prayer, Bible study, fellowship with other believers, journaling, worship, planning and self-evaluation. Re-combine their colors and textures in different ways over a month or a quarter of the year, and you'll see a delightful portrait overlaying the canvass of your life—the image of Jesus Christ. Patience will become less and less a chore to be remembered and fussed with. It'll become more and more who you are. Friends and strangers alike will comment on how you seem to trust God and wait carefully for him. You don't seem as ruffled by the tossing of your life's waves as you used to be. You're slower to anger, more virtuous, a pleasure to be near.

Don't be surprised. You're harvesting the Spirit's fruit! Give God your thanks and praise him.

Appendix A

Use the list below when you need a quick blessing or a bit of guidance as you work through the practice of patience each day. Read the verses in your favorite Bible version, and offer a short prayer to God regarding what the verse says about your current situation. Reflect on the verses in your daily journal.

Nehemiah 9:29-31
Job 6:11-13
Psalm 37:7
Psalm 40:1-3
Proverbs 14:29
Proverbs 15:18
Proverbs 16:32
Proverbs 19:11
Proverbs 25:15
Ecclesiastes 7:8
Isaiah 7:13
Isaiah 38:9-14
Habakkuk 3:16-18
Matthew 18:21-35
Romans 2:3-4
Romans 8:22-25
Romans 9:22-24
Romans 12:9-13

1 Corinthians 13:4-7
2 Corinthians 1:3-7
2 Corinthians 6:4-10
Galatians 5:22-26
Ephesians 4:1-3
1 Thessalonians 5:12-15
1 Timothy 1:15-16
2 Timothy 3:10-15
Hebrews 6:10-12
Hebrews 6:13-15
James 5:7-11
1 Peter 3:17-22
2 Peter 3:8-9
2 Peter 3:14-15
Revelation 1:9-11
Revelation 3:7-10
Revelation 13:5-10
Revelation 14:9-12

Appendix B

Here are a dozen quotations about patience. A good exercise is to read one of them several times. Think about what it says. Ask whether you find it practical or not helpful in your current situation. Why? Why not? Now re-word the quotation to say something you believe will assist you to be more patient today. Write your re-worded statement on a card and carry it with you. Read it several times throughout the day. In the evening, write in a journal how the quotation altered your practice of patience.

Quotations

Patience can avert disaster, but impatience can bring down a whole life.

Anonymous

Have patience with another's blunder, because he has to be patient with yours.

Anonymous

To truly have patience you must not worry.

Anonymous

Patience: Harvesting the Spirit's Fruit

A handful of patience is worth more than a bushel of brains.

Anonymous

Patience: A minor form of despair disguised as a virtue.

Ambrose Bierce

Beware the fury of a patient man.

John Dryden

Adopt the pace of nature: her secret is patience.

Ralph Waldo Emerson

He who can have patience can have what he will.

Benjamin Franklin

We could never learn to be brave and patient if there were only joy in the world.

Helen Keller

Patience is bitter, but its fruit is sweet.

Rousseau

Patience serves as a protection against wrongs as clothes do against cold.

Leonardo da Vinci

All things come to him who waits, provided he knows what he's waiting for.

Woodrow Wilson